# Valorrea Bible Study Guide for Kids

*From Genesis to Revelation: A Complete 20-Chapters Journey Through All 66 Books with Stories, Lessons, and Family Devotions*

*Daniel Shepherd*

## Table Of Contents

Chapter 1: Welcome to Your Bible Adventure! ... 2

Chapter 2: The Adventure Begins: Genesis and Exodus ... 8

Chapter 3: God's Rulebook: Leviticus, Numbers, and Deuteronomy ... 15

Chapter 4: Heroes and Battles: Joshua, Judges, Ruth, and Samuel ... 20

Chapter 5: Kings, Kingdoms, and Exile: Kings, Chronicles, Ezra, Nehemiah, Esther ... 27

Chapter 6: Songs, Wisdom, and Poetry: Job, Psalms, Proverbs, Ecclesiastes, Song of Solomon ... 33

Chapter 7: The Major Prophets Part 1: Isaiah, Jeremiah, Lamentations ... 38

Chapter 8: The Major Prophets Part 2: Ezekiel and Daniel ... 44

Chapter 9: The Minor Prophets Part 1: Hosea through Micah ... 51

Chapter 10: The Minor Prophets Part 2: Nahum through Malachi ... 57

Chapter 11: The Gospels Part 1: Matthew and Mark - Meet Jesus! ... 62

Chapter 12: The Gospels Part 2: Luke and John - Jesus for Everyone! ... 70

Chapter 13: The Church Begins: Acts of the Apostles ... 77

Chapter 14: Paul's Letters Part 1: Romans through Ephesians ... 84

Chapter 15: Paul's Letters Part 2: Philippians through Thessalonians ... 90

Chapter 16: Paul's Letters Part 3: Timothy, Titus, and Philemon ... 96

Chapter 17: Hebrews: Jesus Is Better ... 102

Chapter 18: Living It Out: James and Peter's Letters ... 107

Chapter 19: Love and Truth: John's Letters and Jude ... 113

Chapter 20: The Grand Finale: Revelation and Your Ongoing Journey ... 119

# Chapter 1: Welcome to Your Bible Adventure!

Have you ever opened a book that felt way too big or confusing? That's how many people feel when they first look at the Bible. But here's the exciting news: the Bible might look like one giant book, but it's actually 66 different books bound together—like a library between two covers. You don't have to read it all at once! You can start with adventure stories, poetry, or wise advice—whatever interests you first. Fun Fact: The Bible was written over 1,500 years by more than 40 different authors—including kings, shepherds, fishermen, and prophets!

## What Makes the Bible Special?

The Bible is God's message to humanity—not just an ancient book, but filled with true stories, beautiful songs, wise advice, prophecies, and letters. Even though many authors wrote it over thousands of years, their writings tell one connected story: God's love for people and His plan to rescue us from sin. The Bible has two main parts: the Old Testament and the New Testament. "Testament" means "covenant" or "agreement." Think of it like a promise or a contract between God and people. The Old Testament tells about God's agreement with His people before Jesus came. It shows how God prepared the world for the Savior. The New Testament tells about the new agreement God made through Jesus. It shows how God kept His promise to rescue humanity.

## The Old Testament: Where It All Begins

The Old Testament has 39 books written in Hebrew (the language of ancient Israel). They tell how God created the world, how people turned away from Him, and how God kept working to bring people back. It's a story of God pursuing people who kept running away, but God never gave up on them. You'll meet famous people like Noah, Abraham, Moses, David, and Daniel—real people who faced real challenges and learned to trust God. The Old Testament includes: History Books: These tell the story of God's people, Israel—how God rescued them from Egyptian slavery, gave them laws, led them to the Promised Land, and stayed faithful even when they weren't. Books like Genesis, Exodus, Joshua, Judges, Samuel, and Kings show victories and defeats, faithful kings and terrible kings. Poetry and Wisdom Books: These express feelings and give advice. Psalms contains 150 songs and prayers—from happy celebrations to desperate cries for help. Proverbs gives wise sayings for making good choices. Job explores suffering, Ecclesiastes asks deep questions about life's meaning, and Song of Solomon celebrates love and marriage. Fun Fact: The book of Psalms is like an ancient hymnal—it has 150 songs expressing every emotion you can imagine! Prophets: These books contain God's messages delivered through people like Isaiah, Jeremiah, and Ezekiel. Prophets warned people to turn back to God, comforted them during hard times, and pointed forward to the coming Messiah—the Savior God promised. The Old Testament sets up the Bible's biggest question: How can sinful people have a relationship with a holy God? It shows the problem clearly and promises God has a solution—revealed in the New Testament. Think About It: - The Bible has 66 books written over 1,500 years. What does that tell you about how important God's message is? - Which type of Old Testament book sounds most interesting to you—History, Poetry, or Prophets?

## The New Testament: Jesus Changes Everything

The New Testament has 27 books written in Greek (the common language of that time). It's all about Jesus—who He is, what He did, and what it means for us. Every single book points to Jesus in some way. It begins with four Gospels—Matthew, Mark, Luke, and John—telling about Jesus' life, teachings, miracles, death, and resurrection. Each Gospel writer tells the story from a different angle, giving us a complete picture of Jesus. After the Gospels comes Acts, which tells how Jesus' followers started the church and spread the good news despite facing danger and persecution. You'll read about miracles, dramatic escapes, and bold preaching. Then come the Letters (Epistles)—written by apostles like Paul, Peter, James, and John to churches and individuals. These addressed real problems, answered questions, and gave encouragement, teaching us how to live as Christians and stay strong in faith. Fun Fact: Some New Testament letters are long (like Romans), while others are super short—Philemon is just one chapter! Finally, Revelation ends the New Testament with visions and symbols about how the story ends. The message is clear: Jesus wins! He'll return, defeat evil, and make everything new—a new heaven and earth where God lives with His people forever.

## Why Sixty-Six Books?

You might wonder, "How did these 66 books get chosen?" The 66 books were recognized over time as inspired by God—meaning God guided the authors, ensuring His message came through clearly. These books were carefully examined for authenticity and consistency, fitting together perfectly to tell God's story. Even though written long ago, the Bible is still relevant today. The stories teach about human nature, the wisdom applies to modern life, and God's love remains as true and powerful as ever.

## The Bible Is Like a Library

The Bible contains history, poetry, prophecy, laws, letters, songs, and wise sayings—adventure stories, thoughtful poetry, and wise advice. All these different types work together like instruments in a symphony, giving you God's full message. Even though different parts feel different, they're all connected. The Old Testament sets up the story, showing the problem of sin and promising a Savior. The New Testament completes it, showing how Jesus is that Savior. It all fits together like a beautiful puzzle. Think About It: - If the Bible is like a library, which "section" do you want to explore first—adventure stories, wise advice, or songs and poetry?

## What's This Book Going to Do?

This guide will help you understand all 66 books of the Bible in a simple, fun, and clear way. We'll take a journey through the entire Bible together, from Genesis (where everything begins) to Revelation (where everything is made new). I'll explain what each book is about, who wrote it, when and why it was written, and what you can learn from it. Think of me as your friendly guide on this adventure, pointing out interesting things and helping you understand what you're seeing. Each chapter in this book will cover one or more books of the Bible. I'll tell you the main stories, explain important themes, and help you see how everything connects. By the time you finish this guide, you'll have explored all 66 books and understand the big story the Bible tells. You won't just know facts—you'll understand how the pieces fit together. This guide gives you context and background to really understand what you're reading. It's like having someone who's already been on a hike describe the trail to you. When you wonder "What does this mean?" or "Why is this important?" or "How does this connect to other parts?" this guide answers those questions. You'll discover that the Bible makes a lot more sense when you see the big picture.

## How to Use This Guide

You can read it in order, chapter by chapter, experiencing the Bible's story from creation to the new creation. This is like reading a novel from beginning to end—you get the full flow of the story. Or jump around! If you're curious about the Gospels and want to know about Jesus, skip to Chapters 11-12. Interested in prophets and their messages? Check out Chapters 7-10. Want to know how it all ends? Jump to Chapter 20 about Revelation. It's up to you—this is your journey. Read this guide on your own, setting aside a few minutes each day. Or read it with a parent who can help answer questions and discuss what you're learning. You can also read it with a friend who's curious about the Bible, or as part of a group at church or school. Take your time. There's no rush. Ask questions whenever something confuses you. Think about what you're learning and how it applies to your life. And have fun! This is an adventure, not a boring textbook. I recommend having a Bible nearby as you read. If a story sounds interesting, you can look it up and read it directly from the Bible. This guide helps you understand the Bible, not replace it. The Bible itself is God's Word—this guide just helps you understand it better. The ultimate goal is for you to fall in love with God's Word and read it yourself with confidence and excitement.

## Why Does the Bible Matter?

The Bible tells you the truth about the most important things in life. It answers the biggest questions humans have always asked: Where did we come from? Why are we here? What's wrong with the world? How can it be fixed? Where are we going? The Bible tells you where you came from (God created you on purpose!), why the world is broken (people sinned and turned away from God), how to live a good life (follow God's wisdom and love others), and most importantly, how you can be saved (through faith in Jesus who died for your sins and rose again). The Bible is God's way of speaking to you. Think about that for a moment. The God who made the universe, who created stars and mountains and oceans, who is more powerful than anything we can imagine—He wants to communicate with you through the Bible. When you read it, you're not just reading ancient history. You're hearing from God Himself. He's speaking to you personally. The Bible gives you guidance when you don't know what to do. Should you tell the truth even if it gets you in trouble? The Bible says yes. Should you forgive someone who hurt you? The Bible says yes and shows you how. It gives you comfort when you're sad or afraid, reminding you that God is with you and He cares. It gives you hope when things seem dark, promising that God has good plans for you and that this life isn't all there is. And it reminds you of God's incredible love every single day—love that sent Jesus to die for you, love that never gives up on you, love that will last forever. The Bible introduces you to the most important person who ever lived: Jesus. Everything in the Bible points to Him. He's the hero of the story, the one everything has been building toward. The more you read the Bible, the more you'll know Jesus—and that will change your life. Knowing Jesus isn't just knowing facts about Him. It's having a real relationship with the God who loves you more than you can imagine. Think About It: - How does knowing the Bible is God speaking to you change how you think about reading it?

## You're Ready for This Adventure

I know the Bible can seem big and intimidating, but you're ready for this. You don't need to be a genius or have everything figured out. God doesn't expect you to understand everything right away. He's patient with you and excited to teach you. He's like a kind teacher who loves helping students learn, not a harsh judge waiting for you to make mistakes. This adventure will be amazing. You'll meet heroes like Abraham who trusted God's crazy promises, Moses who stood up to the most powerful ruler on earth, David who went from shepherd boy to king, and Paul who went from persecutor to apostle. You'll read jaw-dropping stories like the parting of the Red Sea where millions of people walked through on dry ground, David defeating the giant Goliath with just a sling and a stone, and Jesus rising from the dead after three days in a tomb. You'll discover wise advice for everyday life—how to choose good friends, how to control your anger, how to make wise decisions. And you'll see over and over that God loves you, cares for you, and has a plan for you. So buckle up! We're about to explore all 66 books of the Bible together. In the next chapter, we'll dive into Genesis and

Exodus and discover how the entire story begins—with God creating a beautiful world and then rescuing His people when things go wrong. Let's go!

Activity Time: Create your own "Bible Map"! Draw a simple path or road with two sections labeled "Old Testament" and "New Testament." On the Old Testament side, draw 3 things you're excited to learn about (like Noah's ark, David and Goliath, or Daniel and the lions). On the New Testament side, draw 3 things about Jesus' story. This will be your adventure map as we journey through the Bible together! For Parents: Before starting the next chapter, ask your child what they already know about the Bible. This helps you understand their current knowledge level and builds on what they've learned at church or home. Share why the Bible is important to you personally—children connect better when they see their parents' genuine faith.

# Chapter 2: The Adventure Begins: Genesis and Exodus

You're about to read the most epic beginning ever told. It starts with darkness and nothingness. Then God speaks, and suddenly there's light blazing into existence, oceans crashing, mountains rising, animals running, and people walking! This is Genesis—the ultimate origin story that actually happened! Genesis tells how God created the world, how sin broke everything, and how God began His plan to fix it. You'll meet Noah who builds a massive boat before a worldwide flood, and a family that trusts God's impossible promises and grows into a nation. Then comes Exodus—the rescue story. God saves His people from Egyptian slavery through miraculous plagues and parts a sea so millions walk through on dry ground! Together, these books show: God creates everything good, and God rescues His people from impossible situations. Fun Fact: The creation story unfolds over six days, and on each day God said "It was good." After creating humans, God said it was "very good"!

## Genesis: In the Beginning

"In the beginning, God created the heavens and the earth" (Genesis 1:1). God existed before anything else. He simply spoke—imagine God's voice booming through nothingness—and the universe came into being! Over six days, God created everything. Day 1: Light. Day 2: Sky. Day 3: Land and plants. Day 4: Sun, moon, and stars. Day 5: Sea creatures and birds. Day 6: Land animals and humans. God made Adam from dust and breathed life into him—suddenly Adam's eyes opened! Then God made Eve from Adam's rib. When Adam woke and saw Eve, he was amazed! God created humans in His image—we can think, create, love, and choose, like God (but He's infinitely more powerful and wise). God gave them beautiful Eden with fruit trees and flowing rivers. Everything was "very good"—no pain, no sadness, no death. Perfect! Day seven, God rested, showing rest is important.

## The Fall: When Everything Broke

God gave one rule: "Don't eat from the tree of knowledge of good and evil." This wasn't harsh—it was a test of trust. Would they believe God knew best? Sadly, they failed. A sneaky serpent (Satan disguised) lied to Eve. "Did God really say you can't eat from any tree?" he asked, twisting God's words. "You won't die! You'll be like God!" The serpent made Eve doubt God. The fruit looked delicious—she took a bite. She gave some to Adam, and he ate too. Everything changed forever. Suddenly they felt shame for the first time. They heard God walking in the garden and hid behind trees, hearts pounding with fear. But you can't hide from God. He called, "Where are you?"—giving them a chance to confess. When confronted, Adam blamed Eve ("The woman you gave me!"), Eve blamed the serpent. Nobody took responsibility. Because of sin, God sent them from the garden. Life became hard. Pain entered. Work became difficult. Worst of all, sin separated them from God. And they would die, just as God warned. But even here, God gave hope—a promise that someone from Eve's descendants would defeat the serpent and crush evil. That promise points to Jesus! God had a rescue plan from the beginning. Think About It: - Adam and Eve had to choose between trusting God or doing things their way. When have you had to make a similar choice?

## Noah: A Fresh Start After the Flood

Fun Fact: Noah's ark was 450 feet long—about as long as one and a half football fields! As people multiplied, they became increasingly evil—violent, selfish, cruel. God's heart filled with pain. He decided to start over with a flood. But one man stood out: Noah. He loved God and lived righteously. God told Noah, "I'm going to flood the earth, but I'll save you. Build a huge ark." God gave exact measurements: 450 feet long! People probably mocked him. "Why build a boat? There's no ocean!" But Noah trusted God and obeyed. When finished, God told Noah to bring his family and two of every animal: giraffes, elephants, mice, lions, snakes, kangaroos, everything! God shut the door tight, and torrential rain began. It rained 40 days and 40 nights without stopping. Water covered everything—even the tallest mountains. Every living thing died except Noah, his family, and the animals inside. After over a year, the waters receded. The ark rested on Mount Ararat. Noah sent birds to check for dry land. A dove returned with an olive leaf—land was appearing! God said, "Come out." Noah worshiped God with sacrifices. God promised never to flood the earth again and put a rainbow in the sky as a sign. When we see rainbows today, we're seeing God's promise!

## Abraham: A Man of Great Faith

God chose one man—Abram (later renamed Abraham). God called him to leave comfortable Ur and go to a land God would show him. Imagine: "Pack up and go... I'll tell you where later!" That takes serious trust! But Abraham obeyed, gathering his family and flocks and walking without knowing where. God made incredible promises. First: "Countless descendants, as many as stars." Try counting stars—you can't! Second: "You'll become a great nation." Third: "Through your family, I'll bless all people." This points to Jesus, who came from Abraham's family! There was one BIG problem: Abraham and Sarah (his wife) didn't have any children, and they were old—really old. Sarah was way past the age of having babies. Years passed. No baby. More years. Still no baby. They got older and older. Abraham must have wondered, "Did I hear God right? How can this happen?" But Abraham believed God anyway. "Abram believed the Lord, and he credited it to him as righteousness" (Genesis 15:6). This is one of the most important verses in the whole Bible! Abraham couldn't earn God's favor by being perfect, but he trusted God's promise, and God considered him righteous because of that faith. Finally, when Abraham was 100 years old (imagine that—being 100!) and Sarah was 90, God kept His promise. They had a son named Isaac. Sarah laughed with joy—after waiting so long, she held her baby boy! From Isaac came Jacob, from Jacob came twelve sons who became the twelve tribes of Israel, and eventually came Jesus. God always keeps His promises, even when we have to wait and even when it seems impossible! Abraham's story teaches us that God keeps His promises even when circumstances look hopeless. Sometimes we have to wait longer than we want. Sometimes God's plan seems impossible. But God is faithful, and trusting Him is never a mistake.

## Joseph: From Pit to Palace

Jacob (Abraham's grandson) had twelve sons. Joseph was his favorite, receiving a special colorful coat. His jealous brothers hated him, especially after Joseph told dreams where they all bowed to him. One day his brothers grabbed him, threw him in a pit, then sold him as a slave to traders heading to Egypt. They dipped Joseph's coat in goat blood and told their father Joseph was dead. Jacob wept while Joseph headed to Egypt in chains. In Egypt, Joseph worked as a slave but was promoted—until his master's wife lied about him and he was thrown in prison. But God was with Joseph. In prison, Joseph interpreted dreams. When Pharaoh had disturbing dreams nobody could interpret, Joseph was brought from prison. Joseph explained: "Seven years of plenty are coming, then seven years of famine. Store food during the good years." Pharaoh put Joseph in charge of all Egypt! Joseph went from prisoner to prime minister. When famine came, Joseph saved many lives—including his family who came to buy food, not knowing the official was their brother! When Joseph revealed himself, his brothers were terrified. But Joseph forgave them, saying, "You intended harm, but God intended it for good to save many lives" (Genesis 50:20). By Genesis's end, the Israelites are living safely in Egypt. Think About It: - How did God use something bad (Joseph being sold into slavery) for something good?

## Exodus: From Slavery to Freedom

Exodus picks up 400 years later. The Israelites have grown into millions! But a new Pharaoh felt threatened and made them slaves, forcing them to make bricks under the hot sun. For 400 years they suffered. They cried to God, who chose Moses to lead them to freedom. Moses had an interesting backstory. Pharaoh ordered all Hebrew baby boys thrown into the Nile. Moses' mother hid him, then put him in a waterproof basket floating among reeds. Pharaoh's daughter found and adopted him. Moses grew up as an Egyptian prince—but knowing he was Hebrew. As an adult, Moses killed an Egyptian who beat a Hebrew slave. When Pharaoh found out, Moses fled to the desert for 40 years. One day, Moses saw a burning bush that wasn't consumed! God spoke: "I've seen my people suffering. I'm sending you to bring them out." Moses protested—"Me? I can't speak well!"—but God insisted, promising to be with him.

## The Ten Plagues: God vs. Egypt's Gods

Moses returned to Egypt and told Pharaoh, "Let my people go." Pharaoh laughed in his face. "Who's your God that I should obey Him? No! The

Israelites are my slaves!" So God sent ten plagues—each one showing His power over things Egyptians worshiped: 1. Water to blood—the Nile turned red and stank 2. Frogs—millions everywhere, even in beds and ovens 3. Gnats—tiny biting insects covering everything 4. Flies—swarms of them everywhere 5. Livestock disease—Egyptian animals died, Hebrew animals lived 6. Boils—painful sores on people and animals 7. Hail—huge hailstones mixed with fire 8. Locusts—insects that ate every plant 9. Darkness—thick darkness for three days (but light where Israelites lived!) 10. Death of the firstborn Each plague showed God's power over things Egyptians thought were gods. But God protected the Israelites from every plague. Before the final plague, God gave instructions: each Israelite family must sacrifice a lamb and put its blood on their doorframes. When God saw the blood, He would "pass over" that house—the firstborn would be safe. This became Passover, still celebrated today. Fun Fact: Passover is still celebrated by Jewish people today, over 3,000 years later! At midnight, the final plague struck Egypt. Every Egyptian firstborn died—from Pharaoh's son to the prisoner's son to the firstborn of animals. Wailing filled Egypt. Pharaoh finally said, "Go! Get out! Take everything and leave!" After 430 years in Egypt, the Israelites were free!

## The Red Sea: An Unforgettable Escape

About 2-3 million Israelites left Egypt with their animals and belongings. They were finally free! But Pharaoh changed his mind and assembled his army—600 chariots plus horses and soldiers—and chased them. The Israelites saw the Egyptian army approaching—dust clouds rising, thundering hooves. They turned and saw the Red Sea ahead. Trapped! Panic spread. "We're going to die! Better to be slaves than die here!" they cried. But Moses said, "Don't be afraid. Watch God rescue you today. He will fight for you!" Then God did the miraculous. Moses stretched his hand over the sea. God sent a powerful wind that blew all night, pushing water back. The water piled up like walls on both sides—a path of dry ground appeared through the sea! Imagine seeing walls of water held back by God's power! The Israelites walked through on dry land. The Egyptians chased them. But once the Israelites reached the other side, God told Moses to stretch his hand again. The waters crashed down with a roar, covering Pharaoh's army. The Israelites were saved! They sang and danced, praising

God. Think About It: - The Israelites felt trapped but God made a way. When have you felt stuck but found a solution?

## Mount Sinai: The Ten Commandments

Three months later, the Israelites reached Mount Sinai. God told Moses to come up. The mountain was covered in smoke and fire, trembling and shaking. Thunder boomed. The people stood back, afraid of God's awesome presence. God gave Moses the Ten Commandments—loving instructions for living well. The first four are about loving God: 1. Don't worship other gods—God alone deserves worship 2. Don't make idols—don't create fake gods 3. Don't misuse God's name—treat His name with respect 4. Keep the Sabbath holy—rest one day a week The next six are about loving others: 5. Honor your parents—respect and obey them 6. Don't murder—life is precious 7. Don't commit adultery—be faithful in marriage 8. Don't steal—respect other people's belongings 9. Don't lie—tell the truth 10. Don't covet—be content with what you have Jesus later summed these up perfectly: "Love the Lord your God with all your heart, soul, and mind, and love your neighbor as yourself." Every commandment fits into these two categories: love God and love others. God also gave detailed instructions for building the Tabernacle—a special tent where His presence would dwell among the people. It had beautiful curtains, golden furniture, and a special inner room called the Most Holy Place where God's presence lived. When it was finished, God's glory filled it like a cloud! God wasn't far away—He was right there with His people, traveling with them through the desert.

## What We Learn

God is the Creator. He made everything good—light, sky, land, plants, animals, people. But sin broke it, bringing pain, death, and separation from God. God makes and keeps promises. He chose Abraham's family to bless the world—ultimately through Jesus, who came from Abraham's line thousands of years later. God is a Rescuer. Just as God rescued Israel from slavery in Egypt with mighty power, Jesus rescues us from slavery to sin and death. The Passover lamb protected Israel from death, pointing forward to Jesus, the Lamb of God, whose blood protects us from sin's consequences. The Red Sea rescue shows God can save us from impossible

situations. The same God who created the world, called Abraham, parted the Red Sea, and rescued Israel loves you today. He's still in the business of rescuing people! When you feel trapped or hopeless, remember: God makes a way!
Activity Time: Draw a picture of the Israelites crossing the Red Sea. Include the walls of water, the people walking through, and Moses with his staff raised high. Write one sentence about how God showed His power. For Parents: Share a "Red Sea moment" from your own life—a time when you felt trapped but God made a way. This helps children see that God is still working miracles today.

# Chapter 3: God's Rulebook: Leviticus, Numbers, and Deuteronomy

Imagine visiting your friend's house for the first time. Before you go inside, they say, "We take our shoes off at the door, and we don't eat in the living room." Are they being mean? No! They're helping you understand how things work so you can fit in. That's what Leviticus, Numbers, and Deuteronomy are like—God's way of teaching His people how to live well and have a good relationship with Him. After escaping Egypt and receiving the Ten Commandments, the Israelites needed more guidance. They needed to know how to worship God, treat each other fairly, and stay healthy as a community. These three books provide that guidance. Behind every rule is God's love and care for His people.

## Leviticus: Learning to Be Holy

Leviticus is a handbook for how to worship God and live as His holy people. "Holy" means "set apart" or "different." God wanted the Israelites to be different from the nations around them—different in a good way, standing out like a light in darkness. Leviticus can feel overwhelming with chapters about sacrifices, skin diseases, food laws, and detailed rules. You might think, "Why do I need to know about ancient animal sacrifices?" But when you understand what's behind these rules, they become fascinating windows into God's character and His plan. Focus on the big themes: Theme #1: Sin is serious. Imagine walking into the Tabernacle courtyard and seeing an Israelite family bringing a lamb—maybe a lamb they'd raised from birth, one their kids had played with. The father would place his hands on the lamb's head, symbolically transferring his family's sin onto the animal. Then the lamb would be killed, its blood shed. The family would watch, hearts heavy, understanding the cost of their sin. The Israelites brought animals—lambs, goats, bulls—as offerings for their sins. Blood had to be shed because sin is that serious. It separates us from a holy God, and there's a real cost to bridge that separation. Every time they saw that sacrifice, they were reminded: sin isn't just breaking rules—it brings death. But here's the amazing part: those sacrifices were temporary, repeated day after day, year after year. They could never fully take away sin—they only covered it temporarily. They were like a preview of something much bigger coming. Jesus became the ultimate sacrifice, the perfect Lamb of God, dying once for all our sins forever. When you read about sacrifices in Leviticus, think about how every single one points forward to Jesus on the cross. Fun Fact: Leviticus 19:2 says "Be holy because I, the Lord your God, am holy." God wasn't asking for perfection—He wanted His people to live differently! Theme #2: God wants us to be holy. God wasn't asking the Israelites to be perfect. He was asking them to be set apart—to live differently than people who worshiped false gods. The same is true today. God wants us to live in a way that reflects His character. Theme #3: God cares about every part of life. Leviticus includes rules about food, clothing, health, relationships, and work. Nothing is too small for God. He wants you to live in a way that honors Him and is good for you. Think About It: - What does it mean to be "set apart" or "different" for God in your daily life?

## Numbers: Wandering in the Wilderness

Numbers is called that because it starts with a census—counting all the Israelite men able to go to war. But it's really the story of Israel's journey from Mount Sinai to the edge of the Promised Land. It's full of grumbling, complaining, disobedience, consequences—and also God's amazing patience, daily provision, and unwavering faithfulness even when His people kept messing up. The Israelites traveled toward the land God promised—a land flowing with milk and honey, a place where they could finally settle down and live in peace. Imagine their excitement as they got closer! When they reached the border, Moses sent twelve spies to check it out—brave men from each tribe who would report back on what they found. Forty days later, the spies returned with incredible news: the land was beautiful and fruitful, even better than they'd hoped! They even brought back grapes so enormous it took two men carrying them on a pole between them! The people gathered around, eyes wide, mouths watering, imagining the abundance waiting for them. But then came the devastating "but." Ten spies said, hearts trembling with fear, "Yes, the land is amazing... but the people there are huge and powerful, like giants! Their cities have massive walls! We felt like tiny grasshoppers next to them. We can't defeat them!" Fear spread through the camp like wildfire. Only two spies—Joshua and Caleb—had faith. They stood up boldly and shouted over the crowd, "Wait! Don't be afraid! Yes, there are challenges, but God is with us! With

God's help, we can absolutely do this! The land is incredible, and God promised it to us. He'll fight for us!" But their voices were drowned out by fear and doubt. Sadly, the Israelites listened to the ten fearful spies instead of trusting God. They panicked, wept all night, and even said, "We should go back to Egypt!" Can you imagine? They'd rather be slaves again than trust God to help them! Because of their lack of faith, God said that generation would not enter the Promised Land. They would wander in the wilderness for 40 years—one year for each day the spies explored. Only their children (and Joshua and Caleb) would enter. Fun Fact: During 40 years of wandering, God provided manna (bread from heaven) every single morning and water from rocks! Those 40 years were tough. The Israelites grumbled constantly. At one point, God sent poisonous snakes as punishment. When people repented, God told Moses to make a bronze snake on a pole. Anyone who looked at it would be healed. Jesus later said this pointed to Him—just as Moses lifted up the snake, Jesus would be lifted up on the cross. Anyone who looks to Jesus in faith will be saved. By the end of Numbers, the 40 years are almost over. The new generation is ready to enter the Promised Land. Think About It: - The Israelites doubted God could help them defeat their enemies. When have you doubted God could help you with something difficult?

## Deuteronomy: Remember and Obey

"Deuteronomy" means "second law." Moses is old now and won't enter the Promised Land (because he disobeyed God once). So he gives speeches to the new generation, reminding them of everything God has done and encouraging them to stay faithful. Deuteronomy repeats many laws but also explains the "why" behind them. One of the most important sections is the Shema (Deuteronomy 6:4-5): "Hear, O Israel: The Lord our God, the Lord is one. Love the Lord your God with all your heart and with all your soul and with all your strength." This became the central prayer of the Jewish people. Moses warns what will happen if they forget God and worship idols. Blessings will come if they obey, but curses if they disobey. God isn't trying to scare them—He's being honest about consequences. Following God's ways leads to a better life. Deuteronomy includes rules about treating others with justice and kindness. God cares deeply about fairness—be honest in business, care for the poor, treat foreigners with respect, and make sure everyone gets a fair trial. Near the end, Moses says something powerful (Deuteronomy 30:19): "I have set before you life and death, blessings and curses. Now choose life, so that you and your children may live." God is giving them a choice: follow Him and live, or turn away and suffer. Finally, Moses climbs Mount Nebo and looks across the Jordan River into the Promised Land. God lets him see it, even though he won't enter it. Then Moses dies, and Joshua becomes the new leader. "Since then, no prophet has risen in Israel like Moses, whom the Lord knew face to face" (Deuteronomy 34:10). Think About It: - Moses told Israel to "choose life." What are some ways you can choose to follow God today?

## Big Themes from These Three Books

God is holy, and He wants His people to be holy too. We're called to live differently because we belong to God. Sin is serious, but God provides a way to deal with it. The sacrifices pointed forward to Jesus, who paid the price for our sin once and for all. God is faithful, even when we're not. The Israelites grumbled and disobeyed repeatedly, yet God never abandoned them. Obedience matters. Following God's commands shows we love and trust Him. Obedience leads to blessing. God cares about how we treat others. God cares about the poor, the foreigner, the widow, and the orphan. Following God means treating everyone with respect and compassion.

## Why Do These Books Matter Today?

These books teach us about God's character—what He values. He values honesty, justice, purity, and love. They show us our need for Jesus. All those laws were impossible to keep perfectly. The Israelites failed repeatedly. We need a Savior—and Jesus is that Savior. They remind us that obedience is an act of love. God's commands aren't burdensome—they're for our good. They show us that God is patient and faithful. Even when we mess up, God doesn't give up on us. These books set the stage for what comes next: the Israelites are finally ready to enter the Promised Land with their new leader Joshua!
Activity Time: Create a "Choice Chart." Draw two paths—one labeled "Choose Life (Follow God)" and one labeled "Turn Away." Under each path, write 2-3 consequences (blessings or struggles). This helps visualize the choices Moses talked about in Deuteronomy 30:19. For Parents:

Discuss with your child how rules in your home aren't meant to be burdensome but to help everyone thrive. Connect this to how God's commands are for our good. Ask: "What's one rule we have that keeps us safe or happy?"

# Chapter 4: Heroes and Battles: Joshua, Judges, Ruth, and Samuel

Picture this: you're standing outside a massive walled city. The walls are so thick and tall they seem impossible to knock down. Inside, enemy soldiers are ready to fight. Your job? Lead God's people to capture this city. But you don't have tanks or explosives—just faith and God's promise that He'll fight for you. After 40 years of wandering, the Israelites are finally ready to enter the Promised Land. Moses has died, and God has chosen Joshua. The books of Joshua, Judges, Ruth, and Samuel are packed with battles, brave heroes, surprising victories, and yes, some failures too. These stories show that God uses ordinary (and sometimes flawed) people to do extraordinary things.

## Joshua: Be Strong and Courageous

The Israelites are camped on the east side of the Jordan River, and the Promised Land is on the other side. Joshua is the new leader, but he's probably nervous. How can he fill Moses' shoes? God knows Joshua needs encouragement, so He tells him three times in the first chapter: "Be strong and courageous." God promises, "I will be with you. I will never leave you or forsake you." That's what Joshua needs to hear—and what we need to hear too. When you face something scary, remember God is with you. Fun Fact: When the priests carrying the Ark of the Covenant stepped into the Jordan River, the water stopped flowing and piled up upstream—just like the Red Sea miracle! Once across the river, the Israelites face their first obstacle: Jericho, protected by massive walls. God has an unusual plan: march around the city once a day for six days. On the seventh day, march around seven times, blow trumpets, and shout. That's it. No battering rams, no weapons. Joshua obeys. On the seventh day, after the seventh lap, the priests blow trumpets, the people shout, and the walls come crashing down! The Israelites rush in and capture the city. It's a stunning victory because they trusted God and followed His instructions—even when they seemed unusual. Joshua leads Israel to conquer many more cities. By the end of the book, Joshua divides the land among the twelve tribes. Before he dies, Joshua challenges the people: "Choose for yourselves this day whom you will serve... But as for me and my household, we will serve the Lord"

(Joshua 24:15). What will you choose? Think About It: - Joshua had to obey God even when His instructions seemed strange (march around a city?). When has obeying God felt confusing but turned out to be right?

## Judges: A Repeating Cycle

After Joshua dies, things get complicated. Judges covers about 300 years. The Israelites settle in the Promised Land but don't fully drive out enemy nations. Instead, they live side by side with people who worship false gods—and slowly start worshiping those gods too. Here's the pattern that repeats in Judges: 1. Israelites turn from God and worship idols 2. God allows enemy nations to oppress them 3. Israelites cry out to God for help 4. God raises up a judge (leader) to rescue them 5. The judge defeats the enemy, and there's peace 6. The judge dies, and the cycle starts again It's frustrating because they keep making the same mistakes! But it shows God's patience and mercy. Every time they cry out, God sends help. The book introduces fascinating judges: Deborah - A wise woman who leads Israel and inspires General Barak to fight. Together they defeat a powerful enemy. Gideon - The Midianites have been oppressing Israel for seven years, stealing their crops and livestock. Israel is so terrified they're hiding in caves! One day, Gideon is secretly threshing wheat in a winepress (instead of out in the open where enemies might see), when an angel appears and says, "The Lord is with you, mighty warrior!" Gideon looks around, thinking, "Who, me? Mighty warrior?" He responds, "If the Lord is with us, why has all this happened? Where are all the miracles our ancestors told us about?" Gideon is discouraged and doubting. But God gives Gideon an assignment: "Go in the strength you have and save Israel from Midian. Am I not sending you?" Gideon protests, "But Lord, my clan is the weakest in Manasseh, and I'm the least in my family!" He feels completely inadequate. But God promises, "I will be with you, and you will strike down all the Midianites." Gideon asks for signs to be sure it's really God—and God patiently gives him signs! Eventually, Gideon gathers an army of 32,000 men to fight the Midianites. But God says, "You have too many men. I don't want Israel to boast that they saved themselves." So God reduces the army—first to 10,000, then down to just 300 men! Against an enemy army of 135,000! The odds are impossible—which is exactly the point. God wants everyone to know He's the one who brings victory. Gideon's 300 soldiers surround the Midianite camp at night. Each soldier has a trumpet, a torch hidden inside a clay jar, and no other weapons. At Gideon's signal, they all blow their trumpets, smash the jars (revealing blazing torches), and shout, "A sword for the Lord and for Gideon!" The sudden noise and lights create chaos. The confused Midianites start fighting each other! They flee in panic, and Israel wins a stunning victory. God used 300 men with trumpets and torches to defeat a massive army—proof that with God, nothing is impossible! Fun Fact: Gideon's 300 soldiers defeated thousands of Midianites using only trumpets, torches, and clay jars—no traditional weapons! Samson - Known for incredible strength (tore apart a lion, killed 1,000 enemies with a donkey's jawbone). But Samson made bad choices. He fell in love with Delilah, who betrayed him. She kept nagging him to reveal his strength's secret. Finally, Samson told her: his long hair, a symbol of his vow to God. Delilah cut his hair while he slept, and Samson lost his strength. His enemies captured, blinded, and enslaved him. But while in prison, Samson's hair grew back. One day, his enemies gathered in a temple to mock him. Samson prayed to God for strength one more time. God heard him, and Samson pushed against the pillars holding up the temple. The building collapsed, killing Samson and thousands of enemies. Even though Samson made mistakes, God still used him to save Israel. Judges ends sadly: "In those days Israel had no king; everyone did as they saw fit" (Judges 21:25). Without godly leadership, people drifted into chaos.

## Ruth: A Beautiful Story of Loyalty and Love

Right in the middle of this dark period, there's a bright spot: Ruth. It's only four chapters but one of the most beautiful stories in the Bible—about loyalty, love, and God's faithfulness. A woman named Naomi, her husband, and their two sons moved to Moab because of famine. While there, the sons married Moabite women named Ruth and Orpah. But then tragedy struck: Naomi's husband died, and both sons died. Naomi was heartbroken. Naomi decided to return to Israel. She told Ruth and Orpah to go back to their families. Orpah left, but Ruth refused. She said, "Where you go I will go, and where you stay I will stay. Your people will be my people and your God my God" (Ruth 1:16). Ruth chose to stay with Naomi and trust Naomi's God. That's incredible loyalty and faith! Ruth and Naomi returned to Bethlehem (where Jesus would be born centuries later). They were poor, so Ruth worked in the fields gathering leftover grain. She worked in a field owned by Boaz—a kind, generous, godly man. When Boaz learned Ruth had been caring for Naomi, he was impressed. He told his workers to leave extra grain for Ruth and keep her safe. Fun Fact: Ruth, a Moabite woman, became King David's great-grandmother—and part of Jesus' family tree! Boaz was a relative of Naomi's late husband, which meant he could act as a "kinsman-redeemer"—marry Ruth to continue the family line. Long story short, Boaz married Ruth. They had a son named Obed, and Naomi was overjoyed! Obed grew up and had a son named Jesse, and Jesse had a son named David—yes, that David, who became Israel's greatest king. And from David's family came Jesus! Ruth's story shows that even in dark times, there are people who remain faithful, kind, and loving. And God can take difficult circumstances and turn them into something beautiful. Think About It: - Ruth showed incredible loyalty to Naomi even when it was hard. Who in your life needs your loyalty and support right now?

## Samuel: From Prophet to Kings

The books of 1 and 2 Samuel tell the story of Israel's transition from judges to kings. A woman named Hannah desperately wanted a child but couldn't have one. She prayed, promising that if God gave her a son, she'd dedicate him to God's service. God answered, and she gave birth to Samuel. When Samuel was old enough, Hannah kept her promise and brought him to the Tabernacle to serve God. One night, young Samuel heard a voice calling his name. He thought it was Eli the priest, but it was actually God! From that moment, Samuel became a prophet—someone who speaks God's words to people. But the people weren't satisfied. They looked at other nations with kings and said, "Give us a king!" Samuel was hurt—and so was God. The people were rejecting God as their king. But God told Samuel to give them what they wanted. Samuel anointed Saul as Israel's first king. Saul was tall, handsome, and impressive. At first, he seemed like a good choice. But Saul had a big problem: he didn't obey God fully. He made excuses and did things his way instead of God's way. Eventually, God rejected Saul as king and told Samuel to anoint a new king. God led Samuel to Jesse's house in Bethlehem. Jesse had eight sons. Samuel met the older sons—tall and strong—but God said no. "People look at the outward appearance, but the Lord looks at the heart" (1 Samuel 16:7). It's not about how you look—it's about your heart. Finally, Jesse brought out his youngest son, David, a teenager who'd been tending sheep. God said, "This is the one." So Samuel anointed David the next king. But David didn't become king right away—he had to wait and face incredible challenges.

## David and Goliath: Faith Over Fear

One of the most famous stories in the Bible happens while David is still a shepherd teenager. The Israelites are at war with the Philistines, camped in a valley with the enemy on the opposite hillside. Every morning and evening for 40 days, a champion named Goliath steps forward from the Philistine ranks. He's massive—over nine feet tall, wearing bronze armor weighing 125 pounds, carrying a bronze javelin and a spear with an iron point weighing 15 pounds. His armor-bearer walks in front of him. Goliath's voice booms across the valley: "Why do you come out and line up for battle? Choose a man and have him come down to me. If he is able to fight and kill me, we will become your subjects; but if I overcome him and kill you, you will become our subjects and serve us!" Then he shouts, "This day I defy the armies of Israel!" The Israelite soldiers—experienced warriors—are absolutely terrified. Nobody dares to fight this giant. The standoff continues day after day, with Goliath mocking them and no one responding. Then David, a teenager, shows up at the camp. His father Jesse has sent him to bring food to his older brothers who are soldiers. David arrives just as Goliath steps forward for his daily taunt. David hears the giant's mocking words and is shocked by what he's hearing—and even more shocked that no one is doing anything about it! He asks the soldiers nearby, "Who is this uncircumcised Philistine that he should defy the armies of the living God?" David's older brother Eliab gets angry: "Why did you come down here? You just want to watch the battle!" But David isn't intimidated. Word reaches King Saul that this young shepherd is asking questions about fighting Goliath. Saul sends for David. When David stands before the king, he volunteers: "Let no one lose heart on account of this Philistine; your servant will go and fight him!" Saul looks at this teenager—ruddy-faced, bright-eyed, probably not much over five feet tall—and says, "You are not able to go out against this Philistine and fight him; you are only a young man, and he has been a warrior from his youth." But David tells Saul his resume: "Your servant has been keeping his father's sheep. When a lion or a bear came and carried off a sheep from the flock, I went after it, struck it and rescued the sheep from its mouth. When it turned on me, I seized it by its hair, struck it and killed it. Your servant has killed both the lion and the bear; this uncircumcised Philistine will be like one of them, because he has defied the armies of the living God. The Lord who rescued me from the paw of the lion and the paw of the bear will rescue me from the hand of this Philistine." Saul finally agrees: "Go, and the Lord be with you." Saul tries to help by offering David his own armor—the king's bronze helmet and coat of armor. David puts them on and tries to walk, but he's not used to them. They're too heavy, too restrictive. "I cannot go in these," David says, "because I am not used to them." So he takes them off. Instead, David chooses five smooth stones from a stream, puts them in his shepherd's bag, and takes his sling in his hand. Then he walks toward the giant. When Goliath sees this teenager approaching with just a stick and a sling, he's insulted and enraged. "Am I a dog, that you come at me with sticks?" he roars. Then he curses David by his gods and threatens, "Come here, and I'll give your flesh to the birds and the wild animals!" The giant is mocking, confident, intimidating. But David shouts back with even greater confidence—not in himself, but in God: "You come against me with sword and spear and javelin, but I come against you in the name of the Lord Almighty, the God of the armies of Israel, whom you have defied! This day the Lord will deliver you into my hands, and I'll strike you down! The whole world will know that there is a God in Israel! All those gathered here will know that it is not by sword or spear that the Lord saves; for the battle is the Lord's, and he will give all of you into our hands!" As Goliath moves closer to attack, David runs quickly toward the battle line to meet him. He reaches into his bag, takes out a stone, loads it in his sling, and swings it with all his might. The stone flies through the air and strikes Goliath right in the forehead—the one spot not protected by armor. The giant crashes forward onto the ground with a thunderous thud. Without even a sword of his own, David runs over, pulls Goliath's massive sword from its sheath, and finishes him off. When the Philistines see their champion is dead, they panic and run! The Israelites surge forward with a great shout, pursuing and defeating the enemy. Israel wins a complete victory—all because one teenager trusted God completely! This story teaches us: faith in God is more powerful than any weapon or enemy. David won because he trusted God completely. When you face giants in your life—bullies, fears, challenges—you can face them with faith, just like David. Think About It: - What "giants" are you facing right now? How can you trust God to help you face them?

## David Becomes King

After defeating Goliath, David becomes famous. King Saul is jealous and tries to kill David multiple times. David has to run and hide for years. But David trusts God and refuses to harm Saul. Finally, Saul dies in battle. David is anointed king, first over Judah and eventually over all Israel. David is a great king—he defeats enemies, captures Jerusalem and makes it his capital, and brings the Ark of the Covenant there with singing and dancing. He writes many Psalms. He's known as "a man after God's own heart." But David isn't perfect. He commits adultery with Bathsheba and arranges for her husband to be killed. When confronted, David repents with a broken heart. God forgives him, but there are still consequences. Despite his failures, David is remembered as Israel's greatest king. God promises that one of David's descendants will rule forever. That promise points to Jesus, the "Son of David," who will reign as King forever!

## What We Learn from These Heroes

God is faithful, even when we're not. The Israelites kept turning away, but God never stopped rescuing them. God uses ordinary people. Joshua was Moses' assistant. Gideon was weak. Ruth was a foreigner. David was a shepherd boy. God can use you, too. Obedience and faith matter. Joshua obeyed God's unusual instructions. David trusted God against Goliath. When we obey and trust God, amazing things happen. Sin has consequences, but God offers forgiveness. Samson and David made terrible choices and suffered. But when they turned back to God, He forgave them. Loyalty and love are beautiful. Ruth's loyalty to Naomi is a sweet example of love. These books show real people with real struggles who served a real God. No matter what giants you face, God is with you. Be strong and courageous!

Activity Time: Draw David facing Goliath. Show David with just a sling and Goliath as a giant with armor. Write one sentence about how faith in God is more powerful than any weapon. For Parents: Share a "Goliath moment" from your life—a time when you faced something that seemed too big but trusted God anyway. Ask your child what their current "Goliath" is and pray together about it.

# Chapter 5: Kings, Kingdoms, and Exile: Kings, Chronicles, Ezra, Nehemiah, Esther

# Chapter 5: Kings, Kingdoms, and Exile Did you know that Israel was once one united kingdom under King David, but it eventually split into two separate nations? It's like if your country suddenly divided into two that didn't get along. This chapter covers dramatic ups and downs in Israel's history—wise and foolish kings, prophets who warned people, exile to foreign lands, and an incredible return home. The books we're looking at are 1 and 2 Kings, 1 and 2 Chronicles, Ezra, Nehemiah, and Esther. Kings and Chronicles tell much of the same history from different perspectives. Together, they paint a full picture of this important time.

## Solomon: The Wisest King

When David gets old, his son Solomon becomes king. One night, God appears to Solomon in a dream and says, "Ask for whatever you want me to give you." Imagine that moment—God Himself offering to give you anything! Solomon could have asked for long life, wealth beyond measure, or victory over all his enemies. But instead, Solomon humbly says, "I'm young and don't know how to lead these people. Please give me wisdom to govern them well and to know right from wrong." God is so pleased with Solomon's humble request that He says, "Because you asked for wisdom instead of selfish things, I'll give you wisdom greater than anyone before or after you. And I'll also give you what you didn't ask for—riches and honor beyond any other king!" When Solomon wakes up, he realizes it wasn't just a dream—God truly spoke to him. Solomon becomes famous worldwide for his wisdom. People travel from distant lands just to hear him speak. He writes thousands of proverbs (wise sayings) and over a thousand songs. He settles disputes with incredible insight. One famous story: two women both claim the same baby is theirs. Solomon says, "Cut the baby in half and give each woman half." One woman agrees, but the other cries out, "No! Give her the baby—just don't hurt him!" Solomon immediately knows she's the real mother because only a true mother would sacrifice everything to save her child. Solomon also builds the magnificent Temple in Jerusalem—a permanent, beautiful house for God to replace the portable Tabernacle. It takes seven years to build with thousands of workers. The Temple is covered in gold, decorated with carved flowers and palm trees, furnished with golden lampstands and tables. When it's finished, Solomon dedicates it with prayer and sacrifices. God's glory fills the Temple so powerfully that the priests can't even stand to minister! For a while, everything seems perfect. Israel is at peace, wealthy, and powerful. But then things go wrong. Solomon marries hundreds of foreign wives who worship false gods. Slowly, Solomon's heart turns away from the Lord. He allows idol worship in Israel. Fun Fact: Solomon's Temple took 7 years to build and was covered in gold—it was one of the most magnificent buildings in the ancient world! Because of Solomon's disobedience, God tells him the kingdom will be torn away from his family—but not during Solomon's lifetime. It will happen during his son's reign.

## The Kingdom Splits in Two

After Solomon dies, his son Rehoboam becomes king. The people ask him to lighten their workload. Rehoboam's older advisors say, "Be kind, and they'll serve you loyally." But Rehoboam ignores them and listens to his young friends instead. He says, "You think my father was harsh? I'll be even harsher!" As a result, ten of the twelve tribes rebel. They form their own nation in the north called Israel (or the Northern Kingdom), choosing Jeroboam as king. Only two tribes—Judah and Benjamin—stay loyal to Rehoboam, forming the Southern Kingdom called Judah. God's people are now divided.

## The Northern Kingdom: A Sad Story

The Northern Kingdom has 19 different kings over about 200 years, and every single one is bad. Not one king leads the people back to God. Instead, they worship idols, mistreat the poor, and ignore God's laws. The first king, Jeroboam, makes two golden calves and tells the people, "Here are your gods!" He sets up false worship centers so people don't have to go to Jerusalem. It's a terrible decision, and future kings follow his bad example. God sends prophets like Elijah and Elisha to warn the Northern Kingdom, but the kings and most people refuse to listen. Finally, God's patience runs out. He allows the Assyrian Empire to conquer the Northern Kingdom in 722 BC. The Assyrians take the people into exile. The ten tribes are scattered and never return as a unified group. Think About It: -

The Northern Kingdom rejected every prophet God sent. Why is it important to listen to godly advice and warnings?

## The Southern Kingdom: A Mixed Story

The Southern Kingdom of Judah lasts longer—about 345 years total. Judah has 20 kings, and while most are bad, a few are good. These good kings try to lead people back to God, tear down idols, and restore proper worship. Hezekiah reopens the Temple (which had been closed) and gets rid of idols. When the Assyrian army surrounds Jerusalem, Hezekiah prays, and God miraculously defeats the Assyrians overnight—an angel strikes down 185,000 soldiers! Josiah becomes king when he's only eight years old! During his reign, workers find a copy of God's Law hidden in the Temple. When Josiah hears it, he realizes how far Judah has strayed. He leads the entire nation in repentance and destroys all idols. Fun Fact: King Josiah was only 8 years old when he became king—younger than most kids in middle school! But after Josiah dies, the next kings return to worshiping idols. God sends prophet after prophet to warn Judah, but they don't listen. Finally, in 586 BC, God allows the Babylonian Empire to conquer Judah. The Babylonians destroy Jerusalem, burn the Temple, and take most people to Babylon as prisoners. It's one of the saddest moments in Israel's history.

## Exile: Far from Home

Imagine being forced to leave your home and everything you know. You're taken to a foreign land where people speak a different language and worship different gods. That's what exile was like. The people felt lost, abandoned, and hopeless. But even in exile, God didn't abandon them. Prophets like Ezekiel and Daniel encouraged the people and reminded them God was still with them. God promised the exile wouldn't last forever. After 70 years, He would bring them back home. And that's exactly what happened!

## Ezra: Returning and Rebuilding

After 70 years in Babylon, the Persian Empire conquers Babylon. The new Persian king, Cyrus, makes a surprising decree: the Jewish exiles are free to return to Jerusalem and rebuild the Temple! About 50,000 Jews make the long journey back. They find the city in ruins with the Temple gone. They immediately rebuild the altar and start offering sacrifices. Then they begin rebuilding the Temple. They face opposition, and construction stops for a while. But prophets like Haggai and Zechariah encourage them. Finally, after years of effort, the Temple is finished. The people celebrate with joy! Later, a priest named Ezra arrives. He's passionate about God's Word. He teaches the people the Law of Moses and calls them to repent from sin. It's a fresh start for God's people. Think About It: - The exiles could have given up, but they kept trusting God. What helps you keep going when something feels too hard?

## Nehemiah: Rebuilding the Walls

Even though the Temple is rebuilt, Jerusalem's walls are still broken down. Without walls, the city is vulnerable to attack. That's where Nehemiah comes in. Nehemiah is a Jewish man living in Persia, working as the king's cupbearer—a trusted position. When he hears Jerusalem's walls are broken, he's heartbroken. He prays and asks the king for permission to rebuild the walls. The king agrees and provides materials! Nehemiah travels to Jerusalem and inspects the damage. He gathers the people: "Come, let's rebuild the wall!" The people respond, "Let's start rebuilding!" Enemies mock and threaten them, but Nehemiah doesn't give up. He organizes workers so half build while the other half stand guard with weapons. Amazingly, the wall is completed in just 52 days! Nehemiah helps Ezra teach the people God's Law. The people weep when they hear it, realizing how far they've strayed. But Nehemiah says, "Don't be sad! This is a day to celebrate. God has brought you home. Rejoice!" The people obey and celebrate with great joy.

## Esther: A Queen Who Saved Her People

The book of Esther is unique—God's name isn't mentioned even once. But His hand is clearly at work, protecting and saving His people. King Xerxes of Persia is looking for a new queen. A Jewish girl named Esther is chosen. She's beautiful, kind, and wise. But the king doesn't know she's Jewish. Haman, a proud official, hates Mordecai (Esther's cousin) because Mordecai refuses to bow to him. Haman plots to kill not just Mordecai but all Jewish people in the empire. He convinces the king to issue a decree that on a certain day, all Jews will be killed. Mordecai sends Esther a powerful message: "Who knows but that you have come to your royal position for such a time as this?" Esther decides to be brave. "I will go to the king, even though it's against the law. And if I perish, I perish." Fun Fact: Approaching the king without being summoned could result in death—even for the queen! After three days of fasting and prayer, Esther approaches the king. Instead of being angry, he's pleased. "What do you want? I'll give you anything, up to half my kingdom!" Esther invites him and Haman to a banquet. That night, the king can't sleep. He reads royal records and learns Mordecai once saved his life but was never rewarded. The next day, he orders Haman to publicly honor Mordecai. At the second banquet, Esther reveals she's Jewish and someone has plotted to kill her people. "Who would dare?" the king demands. Esther points to Haman. The king is enraged. Haman is executed on the very gallows he built for Mordecai! The king issues a new decree allowing Jews to defend themselves. On the day they were supposed to be killed, the Jews fight back and are victorious. The Jewish people celebrate with a new holiday called Purim, still celebrated today. Think About It: - Esther was willing to risk her life to save her people. When have you had to be brave to do the right thing?

## What We Learn from These Books

Sin has consequences. Both kingdoms turned from God and ended up in exile. When people persistently reject God, there are consequences. God keeps His promises, even when we don't. The Israelites broke their covenant repeatedly. But God didn't abandon them. He disciplined but also restored them. Leadership matters. Good kings like Hezekiah and Josiah led people back to God. Bad kings led them into sin. The leaders we follow and become have huge impact. God works behind the scenes. Even when we don't see Him (like in Esther), God is at work, protecting and guiding. Courage and faith change everything. Nehemiah had courage to rebuild the walls. Esther had courage to approach the king. When you have courage and faith, God can use you to do amazing things. God gives second chances. After exile, God brought His people home. He gave them a fresh start. No matter how far you've strayed, God is ready to forgive and give you a new beginning.

Activity Time: Create an "Esther Courage Badge." Draw a crown and write inside it: "For such a time as this" (Esther 4:14). Underneath, write one area where you need courage to stand up for what's right. Keep this badge where you'll see it to remind you God put you where you are for a reason! For Parents: Discuss with your child how Esther was "in the right place at the right time." Help them see that God has placed them in their school, neighborhood, and friendships for a purpose. Ask: "What's one way you can make a difference where God has placed you?"

# Chapter 6: Songs, Wisdom, and Poetry: Job, Psalms, Proverbs, Ecclesiastes, Song of Solomon

# Chapter 6: Songs, Wisdom, and Poetry Have you ever felt so happy you wanted to sing? Or so sad you wanted to cry? Maybe you've felt confused about why something bad happened, or wondered what the point of everything is. Great news: the Bible has entire books that talk about those feelings! The next five books—Job, Psalms, Proverbs, Ecclesiastes, and Song of Solomon—are different from the history books. They're full of poetry, songs, prayers, wise sayings, and honest questions. They show us that God cares about every emotion we feel and every question we ask. These books are sometimes called the "Wisdom Literature" or "Poetry Books" of the Old Testament. They explore big questions about life, suffering, joy, love, and how to live wisely. Let's dive in!

## Job: When Bad Things Happen to Good People

The book of Job tackles one of the hardest questions in life: Why do bad things happen to good people? It's a question we all face when tragedy strikes unexpectedly. Job is described as "blameless and upright"—not perfect, but genuinely trying to live right. He fears God and carefully avoids evil. He's wealthy with seven sons, three daughters, thousands of animals, and many servants. He's respected in his community. Life is really good—until one horrific day when disaster strikes like a series of hammer blows. Imagine Job sitting in his home when a servant runs in, gasping for breath. "Master! Raiders attacked! They took all the oxen and donkeys and killed the servants! I'm the only one who escaped!" Before Job can even process this, another servant bursts in: "Fire fell from the sky and burned up all the sheep and shepherds! Only I survived!" Then another: "Raiders from three directions took all the camels!" And then comes the worst news imaginable. A messenger arrives, tears streaming down his face: "Your children were feasting at your oldest son's house when a mighty windstorm struck. The house collapsed. All ten of your children are dead." Job tears his robe in grief, shaves his head—signs of deep mourning—and falls to the ground. But even in this moment, he worships God: "The Lord gave and the Lord has taken away; may the name of the Lord be praised." Then Satan strikes Job's body with painful sores from head to foot. Job sits among ashes, scraping his sores with broken pottery, utterly miserable. Three friends—Eliphaz, Bildad, and Zophar—hear about Job's suffering and come to comfort him. At first they just sit with him in silence for seven days, which is actually the most helpful thing they do. But then they start talking and make everything worse. They assume Job must have sinned terribly, because they believe suffering is always direct punishment for sin. "Job, just confess whatever you did wrong," they insist. "God is punishing you for something. Think about what secret sin you're hiding!" But Job defends himself passionately: "I haven't done anything to deserve this! You're supposed to be my friends, but you're crushing me with your accusations!" What's amazing about Job is that it shows us it's okay to ask God hard questions and express real emotions. Job pours out his heart to God, even when he's upset, confused, and hurting deeply. He doesn't pretend everything is fine. And God doesn't punish him for his honest questions! But God also reminds Job: God is God, and Job is not. God is infinitely wise and powerful. He created the universe. Sometimes there are reasons for suffering we won't know this side of heaven. Our job is to trust God even when we don't understand. Fun Fact: The book of Job is one of the oldest books in the Bible—it might have been written even before Moses! In the end, God restores Job. He gives him twice as much as he had before. Job's story doesn't answer every question about suffering, but it teaches us that God is with us in our pain, and He's worthy of our trust even when life doesn't make sense. Think About It: - Have you ever asked God "Why?" about something hard in your life? Job shows us it's okay to bring those questions to God.

## Psalms: The Songbook of the Bible

The book of Psalms is like the hymnal of ancient Israel. It contains 150 songs and prayers written over hundreds of years by different authors—King David wrote many, but others were written by Moses, Solomon, and various worship leaders. Psalms covers every emotion you can imagine: joy, sadness, anger, frustration, gratitude, praise, confession, and repentance. If you're feeling something, there's probably a psalm that expresses it. Psalm 23 - "The Lord is my shepherd, I lack nothing." David compares God to a shepherd who takes care of his sheep, leading them to green pastures and protecting them from danger. Even when they walk through dark valleys, they don't have to be afraid because the shepherd is with them. Psalm 139 -

Talks about how God knows everything about you. He knows when you sit and stand. He knows your thoughts before you think them. The psalm says you are "fearfully and wonderfully made." God made you on purpose, with care and creativity. You're not an accident—you're a masterpiece! Psalm 51 - A psalm of confession. David wrote it after he sinned with Bathsheba. He prays, "Have mercy on me, O God, according to your unfailing love... Wash away all my iniquity and cleanse me from my sin." When we mess up, we can come to God honestly, confess our sin, and ask for forgiveness. Fun Fact: Psalm 119 is the longest chapter in the entire Bible with 176 verses—all about how wonderful God's Word is! There are also psalms that express anger or frustration. Some ask God, "How long will you forget me?" These are honest, raw prayers. God can handle our tough questions and strong emotions. Many psalms are songs of praise celebrating God's greatness, His mighty works, His faithfulness, and His love. Psalm 100 says, "Shout for joy to the Lord, all the earth! Worship the Lord with gladness."

## Proverbs: Bite-Sized Wisdom

If Psalms is the songbook, Proverbs is the wisdom handbook. It's filled with short, memorable sayings teaching you how to live wisely. Most were written by King Solomon, known for his incredible wisdom. Proverbs covers all kinds of topics: treating your parents, being a good friend, working hard, controlling your temper, being honest, using words wisely, and much more. Here are some examples: - Proverbs 3:5-6 - "Trust in the Lord with all your heart and lean not on your own understanding; in all your ways submit to him, and he will make your paths straight." Don't try to figure everything out on your own. Trust God and let Him guide you. - Proverbs 15:1 - "A gentle answer turns away wrath, but a harsh word stirs up anger." When someone is angry, responding calmly helps. Responding with anger makes things worse. - Proverbs 16:18 - "Pride goes before destruction, a haughty spirit before a fall." If you're too proud, you're setting yourself up for failure. - Proverbs 9:10 - "The fear of the Lord is the beginning of wisdom." When you respect God and recognize how great He is, that's the starting point for living wisely. Fun Fact: There are 31 chapters in Proverbs—you can read one chapter per day for a month! Proverbs also talks about choosing good friends. Proverbs 13:20 says, "Walk with the wise and become wise, for a companion of fools suffers harm." The people you spend time with influence you. The book emphasizes hard work. Proverbs

6:6-8 says, "Go to the ant, you sluggard; consider its ways and be wise!" Ants are tiny but work hard and plan ahead. We should be like them—diligent and responsible. Think About It: - Which Proverb speaks most to you right now? How can you apply it today?

## Ecclesiastes: The Search for Meaning

Ecclesiastes is written by "the Teacher" (many think it was Solomon in old age). It's a philosophical exploration of life's meaning. The Teacher asks, "What's the point of everything?" The book starts with "Meaningless! Meaningless! Everything is meaningless!" Sounds depressing, right? But the Teacher isn't saying life is worthless. He's saying that if you try to find meaning in temporary things—wealth, pleasure, fame, achievements—you'll end up feeling empty. Those things don't last. The Teacher tries to find meaning in all kinds of things: wisdom, knowledge, huge projects, wealth, and pleasure. But none of it fills the void. Chasing after temporary things is "like chasing after the wind"—you can never catch it. So what's the answer? The Teacher gives it at the end: "Fear God and keep his commandments, for this is the duty of all mankind" (Ecclesiastes 12:13). The key to a meaningful life is knowing God and following Him. Everything else is secondary. Ecclesiastes reminds us that life is a gift from God, and we should enjoy it. Eat good food, spend time with people you love, do satisfying work, and be grateful. But always remember true meaning comes from your relationship with God.

## Song of Solomon: A Love Poem

Song of Solomon (also called Song of Songs) is a beautiful love poem celebrating the love between a husband and wife. It uses vivid, poetic language to describe their affection, admiration, and commitment. Why is a love poem in the Bible? God created love, romance, and marriage. He designed them to be good and beautiful. This book reminds us that romantic love, within marriage, is a gift from God and should be cherished. Some also see Song of Solomon as a picture of God's love for His people. Just as a husband loves his wife deeply, God loves us deeply. He delights in us, treasures us, and is committed to us.

## What We Learn from These Books

It's okay to be honest with God about your feelings. Job and Psalms show us God welcomes our questions, fears, anger, sadness, and joy. Be real with God—He can handle it. Suffering doesn't always mean you did something wrong. Sometimes bad things happen even to people who love God. We live in a broken world. But God is with us in our pain. Wisdom is incredibly valuable. Proverbs teaches us how to make good choices, treat people well, work hard, and live in a way that honors God. True meaning comes from God, not from stuff. Ecclesiastes reminds us that if we try to find fulfillment in temporary things, we'll always feel empty. The only way to find true purpose is through a relationship with God. Love is a gift from God. Song of Solomon celebrates the beauty of love and commitment. God designed us for relationships. Worship is for every emotion. Psalms shows us worship isn't just singing happy songs. It's bringing your whole self—joy, sorrow, confusion, gratitude—to God. Think About It: - Which of these five books speaks most to where you are in life right now?

Activity Time: Write your own short psalm! Pick an emotion you're feeling (happy, sad, worried, grateful) and write 4-5 sentences expressing it to God. You can praise Him, ask Him questions, or thank Him. This is your honest conversation with God, just like the psalm writers had! For Parents: Read Psalm 23 together and ask your child to draw what it describes—a shepherd, green pastures, quiet waters, a valley. Talk about times when your family needed God to be like a shepherd leading you through difficult times. This makes the imagery real and personal.

# Chapter 7: The Major Prophets Part 1: Isaiah, Jeremiah, Lamentations

You're about to meet some of the bravest people in the entire Bible. They're called prophets, and their job was to speak God's messages to the people. Sometimes those messages were hard to hear—warnings about judgment. But often, they were full of hope and promises about a coming Messiah who would save them. That Messiah is Jesus! The books we're looking at—Isaiah, Jeremiah, and Lamentations—are called the "Major Prophets." That doesn't mean they're more important. It just means their books are longer. Isaiah has 66 chapters, and Jeremiah has 52!

## What Is a Prophet?

A prophet is someone God chose to speak His messages to the people. The word "prophet" basically means "spokesman." Prophets were like God's microphone—they delivered His words to the nation. Being a prophet wasn't easy. Often their messages were unpopular. People didn't want to hear they were sinning and needed to change. Sometimes prophets were rejected, mocked, or even harmed. But true prophets stayed faithful to God and spoke the truth, even when it was hard. Prophets also predicted future events. They gave prophecies about the Messiah who would come to save the world. When you read the prophets, you'll notice they talk a lot about a future King, a Suffering Servant, and a time when God would make everything right. All those prophecies point to Jesus.

## Isaiah: The Prophet of the Messiah

Isaiah is one of the most important books in the Old Testament. It's quoted more in the New Testament than any other prophetic book because Isaiah talks so much about Jesus! Isaiah lived around 700 BC, during the time when the Assyrian Empire was threatening Israel. Isaiah's book has two main parts. The first part (chapters 1-39) focuses on judgment and warnings. God is holy, and sin is serious. But even here, there are glimpses of hope. The second part (chapters 40-66) is filled with comfort and promises. Isaiah speaks about a future when God will rescue and restore

His people. He talks about a Messiah who will bring salvation not just to Israel, but to the whole world.

## The Holy, Holy, Holy Vision

In chapter 6, Isaiah has a dramatic, life-changing vision of God sitting on a throne—high and exalted, filling the temple with the train of His robe. This isn't a gentle scene. It's overwhelming, majestic, terrifying in its glory. Angels called seraphim surround the throne, each with six wings. With two they cover their faces (too holy to look directly at God), with two they cover their feet (in humility), and with two they fly. The seraphim call out antiphonally to one another in thunderous voices: "Holy, holy, holy is the Lord Almighty; the whole earth is full of his glory!" Saying it three times emphasizes God's complete, perfect, absolute holiness. The sound is so powerful that the doorposts and thresholds shake, and the temple fills with smoke—like when God's presence filled the Tabernacle in Moses' time. When Isaiah sees God's glory and holiness, he's not excited or proud to have seen this vision. He's absolutely terrified and overwhelmed. He cries out in despair, "Woe to me! I am ruined! I'm a man of unclean lips, and I live among a people of unclean lips, yet my eyes have seen the King, the LORD Almighty!" Isaiah suddenly realizes how sinful he is compared to God's perfection. He feels like he's going to die because he's seen God in all His holiness and knows he's not worthy. But then one of the seraphim flies to Isaiah, carrying a live coal from the altar with tongs. The angel touches Isaiah's mouth with the burning coal—imagine how that must have felt!—and says, "See, this has touched your lips; your guilt is taken away and your sin atoned for." In an instant, Isaiah is cleansed and forgiven. That burning coal represents purification. Then Isaiah hears God's voice: "Whom shall I send? And who will go for us?" And now, cleansed and forgiven, Isaiah eagerly responds, "Here am I. Send me!" This vision teaches us that God is incredibly holy—far more than we can imagine—and it's only because of His grace that sinful people like us can come near to Him. We need cleansing before we can serve God, and He's the one who provides it. Fun Fact: Isaiah's name means "The LORD saves"—which perfectly describes his message about the coming Messiah!

## Prophecies About Jesus

Isaiah is filled with prophecies about Jesus: Isaiah 7:14 - "The virgin will conceive and give birth to a son, and will call him Immanuel." This was fulfilled when Jesus was born to the virgin Mary. "Immanuel" means "God with us"! Isaiah 9:6 - "For to us a child is born, to us a son is given... And he will be called Wonderful Counselor, Mighty God, Everlasting Father, Prince of Peace." This is one of the most famous prophecies about Jesus! Isaiah 53 - This is one of the most amazing chapters in the Old Testament. It describes a "Suffering Servant" who will be despised and rejected, who will carry our sorrows, and who will be pierced for our transgressions. It says, "By his wounds we are healed." This is a detailed description of what Jesus would do on the cross. Isaiah wrote this about 700 years before Jesus was born! Isaiah 61:1-2 - "The Spirit of the Sovereign Lord is on me, because the Lord has anointed me to proclaim good news to the poor." When Jesus started His ministry, He read this passage and said, "Today this scripture is fulfilled in your hearing" (Luke 4:21). Isaiah also talks about a new heaven and new earth where there will be no more crying or pain. That promise will be fulfilled in the future!

## Trusting God, Not Human Power

One big theme in Isaiah is trust. Judah was surrounded by powerful enemy nations. Leaders were tempted to make alliances with other countries instead of trusting God. Isaiah repeatedly told them, "Trust God! He's the one who will save you!" Isaiah 40:31 is beautiful: "But those who hope in the Lord will renew their strength. They will soar on wings like eagles; they will run and not grow weary, they will walk and not be faint." When you put your hope in God, He gives you strength to keep going. Think About It: - Isaiah trusted God even when his messages were unpopular. When have you had to trust God even when it was hard?

## Jeremiah: The Weeping Prophet

Jeremiah is known as "the weeping prophet" because he literally cried and mourned over the sins of his people and the coming judgment he had to announce. Imagine having to tell people you love that disaster is coming, and they refuse to listen. That was Jeremiah's life. He lived about 100 years after Isaiah, around 600 BC. His ministry overlapped with the final, tragic years of Judah before the Babylonians destroyed Jerusalem and the Temple. Jeremiah had one of the toughest prophet jobs in history. His message was: "Jerusalem will be destroyed, and you'll be taken into exile." Nobody wanted to hear that! Instead of listening and repenting, the people attacked Jeremiah. They accused him of being a traitor and a liar. "How dare you say God will let our enemies defeat us!" They beat him, put him in stocks (like being locked in place in public so people could mock you), threw him into a cistern (a muddy well) and left him to die slowly, sinking in the mud (though he was rescued by a kind Ethiopian official named Ebed-Melek). Despite all this persecution and suffering, Jeremiah stayed faithful to God and kept speaking God's truth even when it cost him everything.

## Jeremiah's Calling

When God first called Jeremiah, he was young and scared. He said, "I do not know how to speak; I am too young." But God told him, "Do not say, 'I am too young.' You must go to everyone I send you to and say whatever I command you. Do not be afraid, for I am with you and will rescue you" (Jeremiah 1:7-8). God promised to be with Jeremiah and protect him. And even though Jeremiah faced rejection and suffering, God kept that promise. Jeremiah's story reminds us that God can use anyone—even young people—if they're willing to obey Him. Fun Fact: Jeremiah was called to be a prophet when he was probably a teenager—not much older than you!

## Hard Messages and Hopeful Promises

Most of Jeremiah contains warnings about judgment. He told the people that because they had worshiped idols, God was going to allow the Babylonians to conquer them. He urged the people to repent, but they refused. Jeremiah watched as his prophecies came true. The Babylonians destroyed Jerusalem, burned the Temple, and took most people as prisoners. It was heartbreaking. But even in the midst of judgment and sorrow, Jeremiah gave messages of hope. One of the most beautiful passages is Jeremiah 29:11: "For I know the plans I have for you, plans to prosper you and not to harm you, plans to give you hope and a future." Even though the people were going into exile, God promised He hadn't forgotten them. After 70 years, He would bring them back home. Jeremiah also prophesied about a "new covenant." He said, "I will put my law in their minds and write it on their hearts. I will be their God, and they will be my people" (Jeremiah 31:33). This new covenant was fulfilled through Jesus! Now, through faith in Jesus, we can have a personal relationship with God, and the Holy Spirit lives inside us. Think About It: - God told Jeremiah, "You're not too young." What's one way you can serve God right now, regardless of your age?

## Lamentations: Songs of Sorrow

Lamentations is a short book of five chapters written (most likely by Jeremiah) after Jerusalem was destroyed. "Lament" means to express deep sorrow or grief. This book is a collection of poems expressing grief over the destruction of Jerusalem and the suffering of God's people. Lamentations doesn't hold back. It describes the horrors of the siege, the famine, the destruction of the Temple, and the pain of exile. It's raw and honest. The writer asks, "Why has this happened? How long will this last?" But even in all this sorrow, there's hope. Lamentations 3:22-23 says, "Because of the Lord's great love we are not consumed, for his compassions never fail. They are new every morning; great is your faithfulness." Even when everything else is falling apart, God's love and faithfulness remain. His mercies are new every morning. Every day is a fresh start! Lamentations teaches us that it's okay to grieve. It's okay to cry and express your pain to God. He doesn't expect you to pretend everything is fine. But even in your grief, you can hold onto hope. God's love never fails. Think About It: - "God's mercies are new every morning" means you get a fresh start every day. How does that change the way you think about yesterday's mistakes?

## Connecting the Dots

Isaiah, Jeremiah, and Lamentations all fit together: Sin has consequences. God is patient and loving, but He's also just. When people persistently reject Him, there are consequences. God is faithful even when we're not. Even though the people sinned, God never completely abandoned them. He promised to restore them, and He did. God's plan includes a Messiah. Isaiah's prophecies show us that God had a rescue plan all along—Jesus! It's okay to be honest with God. Jeremiah and Lamentations show we can be real with God about our pain, confusion, and sorrow. Hope is always available. No matter how dark things get, there's always hope in God. His love never fails.

Activity Time: Create a "Fresh Start" morning reminder. On a card, write "God's mercies are new every morning!" (Lamentations 3:23). Decorate it with a sunrise. Put it where you'll see it first thing each morning to remember that today is a brand-new start, no matter what happened yesterday. For Parents: Discuss with your child what "God's mercies are new every morning" means for your family. Share a time when you needed a fresh start, and God gave you one. This helps children understand that mistakes aren't final—God always offers another chance.

# Chapter 8: The Major Prophets Part 2: Ezekiel and Daniel

Picture this: you're standing in a valley filled with dry bones—thousands of skeletons scattered everywhere. Suddenly, God speaks to the bones, and they start rattling and coming together! Muscles and skin form, and they come back to life, standing up as a vast army. Sounds like something from a movie, but it's actually a vision from Ezekiel! Or imagine this: you're thrown into a den of hungry lions for praying to God. The lions circle around you, jaws ready. But God shuts their mouths, and they don't touch you. You spend the whole night with the lions and walk out the next morning without a scratch. That's a true story from Daniel! Ezekiel and Daniel are the last two Major Prophets, and their books are filled with incredible visions, miraculous stories, and powerful messages. Both prophets lived during the Babylonian exile, when God's people were far from home and feeling hopeless. But they reminded everyone that God is still in control, even in the darkest times.

## Ezekiel: The Prophet of Visions

Ezekiel was a priest taken into exile in Babylon in 597 BC (about 10 years before Jerusalem was completely destroyed). While in exile, God called Ezekiel to be a prophet. His job was to help the exiled Jews understand why they were in exile and what God's plans were for the future. Ezekiel's book is full of symbolic visions and dramatic actions. Even though the Temple was destroyed and they were far from Jerusalem, God was still with them. His presence wasn't limited to one place.

## The Vision of God's Glory

Ezekiel's calling starts with one of the wildest visions in the entire Bible. In chapter 1, he sees the heavens open. He describes seeing four living creatures with four faces (human, lion, ox, and eagle), wheels within wheels covered with eyes, and a throne with a figure surrounded by blazing light. It's hard to picture! But the point is clear: God is awesome, powerful, and glorious beyond anything we can imagine. Later, Ezekiel sees a vision of God's glory leaving the Temple in Jerusalem. The people thought God's presence was tied to the Temple, but God's glory left because they had filled the Temple with idols. Sin drives God's presence away. But here's the good news: later Ezekiel sees God's glory returning to a new, restored Temple. God won't stay away forever! Fun Fact: Ezekiel's vision of the four living creatures is similar to what John sees in the book of Revelation—connecting the Old Testament to the New!

## Ezekiel's Dramatic Actions

God often told Ezekiel to do unusual things to communicate messages. God told Ezekiel to lie on his left side for 390 days and then on his right side for 40 days. Each day represented a year of Israel's and Judah's sin. That's a long time to lie on your side! Another time, God told Ezekiel to pack his bags and dig through a wall to symbolize the coming exile. Ezekiel also shaved his head and divided the hair into three parts—one to burn, one to chop with a sword, and one to scatter in the wind. This symbolized what would happen to Jerusalem's people. These actions probably seemed strange, but they were meant to grab attention and make people think about God's message. Sometimes God uses unusual methods to get our attention!

## The Valley of Dry Bones

One of the most famous passages in all of Scripture is Ezekiel's vision of the valley of dry bones in chapter 37. Imagine this scene: God's Spirit takes Ezekiel to a valley—a huge, open plain—filled with bones. Not just a few bones, but thousands upon thousands of skeletons scattered everywhere you look. They're very dry, bleached white by the sun, clearly dead for a long, long time. There's no life here at all, just death and hopelessness stretching in every direction. God leads Ezekiel back and forth among the bones and then asks him a stunning question: "Son of man, can these bones live?" It's almost like God is testing him. Can the absolutely impossible happen? Ezekiel, showing great wisdom, doesn't say yes or no. Instead he answers, "Sovereign Lord, you alone know." He's basically saying, "I have no idea, but if anyone can do this, it's You!" Then God gives Ezekiel an unusual command: "Prophesy to these bones and say to them, 'Dry bones, hear the word of the Lord!'" So Ezekiel, standing in this valley of death, starts preaching to dead bones. And as he speaks God's word, something incredible happens. There's a noise—a rattling sound. The bones start shaking and moving! They begin coming together, bone connecting to bone. Then tendons appear, attaching the bones. Muscles form over the skeletons. Skin covers the bodies. Before Ezekiel's eyes, the scattered bones become complete bodies lying on the ground. But here's the thing: they're still not alive. They look like bodies, but there's no breath in them. They're corpses, not living people. Then God tells Ezekiel to prophesy to the breath: "Come, breath, from the four winds and breathe into these slain, that they may live!" When Ezekiel obeys, breath enters the bodies. They come to life and stand up on their feet—a vast army, countless people alive again! What does this mean? God explains: "These bones are the people of Israel. They say, 'Our bones are dried up and our hope is gone.' But I will bring you back to life. I will put my Spirit in you, and you will live." Even though the people felt dead and hopeless in exile, God promised to bring them back to life and back to their land. And He did! This vision also points forward to the ultimate resurrection when Jesus returns. One day, God will raise all His people from the dead! Think About It: - The dry bones looked completely hopeless, but God brought them back to life. What situation in your life feels hopeless but God could change?

## The Promise of a Good Shepherd

In chapter 34, God condemns the bad shepherds (leaders) of Israel who cared more about themselves than about the people. But God promises to be the Good Shepherd Himself. He'll search for His sheep, rescue them, and care for them. This is a prophecy about Jesus! Jesus called Himself the Good Shepherd (John 10:11). He cares for His sheep, protects them, and lays down His life for them.

## Daniel: The Prophet in the Palace

While Ezekiel was prophesying to the exiles, Daniel was living in the royal palace. Daniel was taken to Babylon as a teenager during the first wave of exiles (about 605 BC). He was smart, handsome, and talented, so he was chosen to be trained in the Babylonian court. He eventually rose to a high position, serving under multiple kings. Daniel's book is divided into two parts. The first half (chapters 1-6) tells stories about Daniel and his friends standing firm in their faith despite pressure to compromise. The second half (chapters 7-12) contains visions about future kingdoms and the coming Messiah.

## Daniel and His Friends Stand Firm

When Daniel and his friends (Shadrach, Meshach, and Abednego) first arrive in Babylon, they're told to eat the king's rich food and wine. But this food has been offered to idols, which goes against God's commands. Daniel respectfully asks if they can eat vegetables and water instead. The official is worried they'll look weak, but Daniel suggests a test: "Let us eat vegetables and drink water for ten days, and then compare us with the other young men." At the end of ten days, Daniel and his friends look healthier than everyone else. God honors their faithfulness! This teaches us: when you're faced with pressure to compromise your faith, stand firm. Be respectful and wise, but don't give in. God will honor your faithfulness. Fun Fact: Daniel's name means "God is my judge"—fitting for someone who stood firm in faith regardless of what others thought!

## The Fiery Furnace

Later, King Nebuchadnezzar builds a huge golden statue—90 feet tall, probably of himself—and sets it up on a plain where everyone can see it. He sends out a decree commanding all officials, nobles, and people to come to its dedication ceremony. When the music plays—harps, lyres, zithers, and all kinds of instruments—everyone must fall down and worship the statue. Anyone who refuses will be thrown immediately into a blazing furnace. The threat is clear and terrifying. The day arrives. Thousands of people gather. The music starts playing, and like a wave, everyone falls to their knees, faces to the ground, worshiping the golden statue. Everyone, that is, except three young men: Shadrach, Meshach, and Abednego. While thousands bow, they remain standing, visible to everyone around them. Imagine the courage that took! Officials who are jealous of these three Jewish men rush to the king. "Your Majesty, there are some Jews—Shadrach, Meshach, and Abednego—whom you've put in charge of the province of Babylon. They pay no attention to you! They neither serve your gods nor worship the gold image you've set up." Nebuchadnezzar is absolutely furious. His face contorts with rage. He orders the three men brought before him. He gives them one more chance, trying to control his anger: "Is it true? When you hear the music, will you fall down and worship the statue I made? If you do, good. But if you don't, you'll be thrown immediately into the blazing furnace. Then what god will be able to rescue you from my hand?" He's basically challenging their God. The three friends don't even hesitate. Their answer is one of the most powerful statements of faith in the entire Bible: "King Nebuchadnezzar, we don't need to defend ourselves before you in this matter. If we're thrown into the blazing furnace, the God we serve is able to deliver us from it, and he will deliver us from Your Majesty's hand. But even if he does not, we want you to know, Your Majesty, that we will not serve your gods or worship the image of gold you've set up." Did you catch that incredible faith? "Our God can save us. We believe He will. But even if He chooses not to, even if we die in that furnace, we STILL won't bow down." They're willing to die rather than compromise their faith. That's real commitment! The king orders the furnace heated seven times hotter. The three men are thrown into the fire. It's so hot that the soldiers who throw them in are killed by the flames. But then something amazing happens. The king looks into the furnace and sees four men walking around unharmed. "But I see four men," the king says, "and the fourth looks like a son of the gods!" God sent an angel to protect them! When they emerge, they don't even smell like smoke. Their hair isn't singed, their clothes aren't scorched, and they're completely unharmed. Everyone is amazed. King Nebuchadnezzar praises God! Think About It: - Shadrach, Meshach, and Abednego were willing to be faithful even if God didn't save them. When have you had to obey God even when you weren't sure how things would turn out?

## Daniel in the Lions' Den

Years pass. Babylon falls to the Persians, and Daniel now serves under the new Persian king, Darius. By this time Daniel is probably in his eighties, but he's still sharp and capable. Daniel does his job so exceptionally well—with such integrity and competence—that King Darius plans to put him in charge of the entire kingdom, over all the other officials. This makes the other officials insanely jealous. They desperately want to find something to accuse Daniel of—some mistake, some corruption, some failure. They search and search but find nothing. Daniel is faithful and trustworthy. Finally, they say to each other, "We'll never find any basis for charges against this man Daniel unless it has something to do with the law of his

God." So they hatch a devious plan. They come to the king as a group and flatter him: "Your Majesty, live forever! We all agree—all the royal administrators, prefects, satraps, advisers and governors—that you should issue a decree: for the next 30 days, anyone who prays to any god or human except you, Your Majesty, should be thrown into the den of lions. Now, Your Majesty, issue the decree and put it in writing so it can't be altered, according to the law of the Medes and Persians, which cannot be repealed." King Darius, not realizing this is a trap for Daniel, agrees and signs the decree. Once signed, according to Persian law, it absolutely cannot be changed—not even by the king himself. When Daniel hears about the new law, does he stop praying? Does he hide and pray in secret where no one can see? Nope! Daniel goes home to his upstairs room, opens his windows facing toward Jerusalem (the direction Jews prayed), kneels down, and prays to God three times a day—exactly like he's always done. He doesn't make a scene, but he doesn't hide either. His relationship with God is more important than any law or threat. The officials are watching and waiting. They catch Daniel praying and immediately report him to the king. King Darius is upset—he likes Daniel—but the law can't be changed. Daniel must be thrown to the lions. Before Daniel is thrown in, the king says, "May your God, whom you serve continually, rescue you!" The king spends the whole night unable to sleep. At dawn, he rushes to the den and calls out, "Daniel, has your God been able to rescue you?" Daniel answers, "My God sent his angel, and he shut the mouths of the lions. They have not hurt me!" The king is overjoyed. Daniel doesn't have a single scratch. The king orders that the men who accused Daniel be thrown into the den instead. King Darius issues a decree that everyone should fear and reverence the God of Daniel. This story is so encouraging! Daniel stayed faithful even when it was dangerous. And God protected him miraculously. When you face pressure to stop praying or following God, remember Daniel. Be faithful, and trust that God is with you.

## Daniel's Visions

The second half of Daniel contains visions about future events. Daniel sees visions of four great beasts representing kingdoms that will rise and fall. He receives prophecies about a coming ruler who will oppose God but will ultimately be defeated. One of the most important prophecies is in Daniel 9, where the angel Gabriel tells Daniel about "seventy sevens." This prophecy gives a timeline for when the Messiah will come, be cut off (crucified), and when the Temple will be destroyed. It's an incredibly accurate prophecy pointing to Jesus. Daniel also has visions of the end times—a time of great trouble followed by God's ultimate victory and resurrection of the dead. The main message is clear: God is in control of history, and He will ultimately defeat evil and establish His kingdom forever. Think About It: - Daniel's visions show that God knows the future and is in control. How does knowing God is in control help you when life feels uncertain?

## What We Learn from Ezekiel and Daniel

God's presence isn't limited to one place. Even though the Temple was destroyed, God was still with them. You can worship God anywhere. His presence goes with you. God can bring dead things back to life. The valley of dry bones reminds us nothing is too hopeless for God. He can take what looks dead and breathe new life into it. Stand firm in your faith, even under pressure. Daniel and his friends faced intense pressure to compromise, but they stood firm, and God honored their faithfulness. God protects His people. Whether it's in a fiery furnace or a lions' den, God can protect you miraculously. That doesn't mean you'll never face hard times, but God is with you. God is in control of history. Kings and kingdoms rise and fall, but God's plan never changes. He's sovereign over everything. Hope is coming. Both Ezekiel and Daniel point forward to when God will restore His people, send the Messiah, and establish His kingdom forever. That Messiah is Jesus!

Activity Time: Create a "Stand Firm" reminder. Draw a picture of Daniel in the lions' den or the three friends in the fiery furnace. Write on it: "Stand Firm in Faith!" Put it somewhere you'll see it when you face pressure to compromise your beliefs. For Parents: Discuss with your child a time when standing up for what's right was hard. Share how you handled it and what helped you stay strong. Connect this to how Daniel and his friends stayed faithful. Ask: "What's one area where you feel pressure to compromise? How can we pray about that together?"

# Chapter 9: The Minor Prophets Part 1: Hosea through Micah

# Chapter 9: The Minor Prophets Part 1 The last twelve books of the Old Testament are sometimes called "The Book of the Twelve" because in ancient times, they were all written on one scroll! These twelve books are called the Minor Prophets—not "minor" in importance, just shorter than the Major Prophets. Each one packs a powerful message about God's love, justice, mercy, and faithfulness. In this chapter, we'll explore the first six: Hosea, Joel, Amos, Obadiah, Jonah, and Micah. Each prophet has a unique personality and message, but they all point us back to the same truths about God.

## Hosea: A Prophet's Heartbreaking Love Story

Hosea's book is one of the most emotional and heart-wrenching in the entire Bible. God gives Hosea a command that must have sounded absolutely crazy: "Go, marry a promiscuous woman and have children with her, for like an adulterous wife this land is guilty of unfaithfulness to the Lord." Imagine hearing God tell you to marry someone you know will break your heart! So Hosea obeys. He marries a woman named Gomer, and they have children together. For a while, maybe things seem okay. But then Gomer's unfaithfulness becomes clear. She leaves Hosea for other lovers. She abandons their family, pursuing other relationships. Hosea experiences the devastating pain of betrayal and abandonment. His heart is completely broken. But here's why God asked Hosea to do this: Hosea's painful, heartbreaking marriage is a living picture—a real-life illustration—of Israel's relationship with God. Just as Gomer is unfaithful to Hosea, Israel has been unfaithful to God. The people worship idols—statues of Baal and Asherah—bowing down to false gods made of wood and stone. They break God's commands over and over. They've broken their covenant with God, just like a spouse who cheats on their partner and walks away. But here's the absolutely amazing part, the part that shows us God's incredible love: even though Gomer has left Hosea and ends up in slavery (probably sold because of debts or by someone who used her), God tells Hosea, "Go, show your love to your wife again, though she is loved by another and is an adulteress. Love her as the Lord loves the Israelites." So Hosea goes and finds Gomer. He pays fifteen shekels of silver and some barley to buy her freedom—to redeem her out of slavery. He brings her home and restores her as his wife. This is a stunning picture of God's love for Israel and for us! Even when we're unfaithful, even when we reject Him and chase after other things, God still loves us. He pursues us. He pays the price to redeem us—and that price was Jesus' death on the cross. He brings us home. Hosea 11:8 shows God's heart: "How can I give you up, Ephraim? How can I hand you over, Israel? My heart is changed within me; all my compassion is aroused." God's love is relentless. Fun Fact: Hosea's name means "salvation"—which perfectly describes God's redeeming love for His people! Think About It: - Hosea redeemed Gomer even after she left him. How does this show us what God's love is like?

## Joel: The Day of the Lord

Joel is a short book—only three chapters—but delivers a powerful message. Joel prophesies during a devastating plague of locusts that destroyed all crops. It's a disaster. Joel uses this as a picture of something even worse: the coming "Day of the Lord"—a day of judgment when God will punish sin. Joel warns the people to repent. He says, "Rend your heart and not your garments. Return to the Lord your God, for he is gracious and compassionate, slow to anger and abounding in love" (Joel 2:13). "Rend your heart" means to truly repent from the inside, not just put on a show. But Joel also gives a beautiful promise. After judgment, God will restore what was lost. He'll pour out His Spirit on all people—young and old, men and women. This prophecy was fulfilled on the Day of Pentecost when the Holy Spirit came upon the disciples!

## Amos: The Prophet of Justice

Amos was an ordinary man—a shepherd who took care of sheep and a farmer who cultivated sycamore fig trees. He wasn't a trained prophet or priest from a prophetic school. He wasn't from a royal or priestly family. He was just a working man from the small village of Tekoa in Judah. But God called him to deliver a powerful message to the Northern Kingdom of Israel, the wealthy and prosperous kingdom to the north. Amos travels to Israel and is shocked by what he sees. The nation is experiencing economic prosperity—the rich are getting richer—but they're doing it by stepping on the poor and vulnerable. They're selling honest people into slavery over tiny debts. They're trampling the needy and cheating customers with dishonest scales. They're accepting bribes in court. The wealthy lounge on expensive couches, eat fancy food, drink wine by the bowlful, and cover themselves with expensive perfumes—while not caring at all about the suffering around them. And what's worse, they're still going to the religious festivals! They're bringing sacrifices and offerings to God, singing worship songs, going through all the religious motions. But their hearts are completely far from God. It's all just an empty show. Amos's message is all about justice and righteousness. He delivers one of the most powerful verses in Scripture: "But let justice roll on like a river, righteousness like a never-failing stream!" (Amos 5:24). Imagine a river that never stops flowing, constantly bringing fresh water. That's what God wants—constant, consistent justice and righteousness, not just occasional religious performances. God doesn't just want religious rituals—He wants His people to actually live justly, treat others fairly, and care for the poor and vulnerable. Amos warns that judgment is coming if they don't repent. And sadly, his prophecy came true. The Northern Kingdom was conquered by Assyria not long after. But Amos ends with a promise: God will restore Israel. He'll rebuild what was torn down and plant His people in their land, never to be uprooted again. Fun Fact: Amos was a shepherd from a small town called Tekoa—proving God can use anyone, no matter how "ordinary" they seem! Think About It: - Amos says God wants justice and righteousness, not just religious rituals. What's one way you can show justice and fairness this week?

## Obadiah: The Shortest Book in the Old Testament

Obadiah is the shortest book in the Old Testament—just one chapter with 21 verses! Obadiah's message is directed at Edom, which was descended from Esau (Jacob's twin brother). The Edomites should have helped their relatives when Jerusalem was destroyed. Instead, they stood by, gloated, and took advantage of the situation. Obadiah's message: God will judge Edom for their pride and cruelty. "As you have done, it will be done to you" (Obadiah 1:15). What goes around comes around. But Obadiah also gives hope to Israel. God will restore His people, and His kingdom will be established. Evil won't have the final say—God will.

## Jonah: The Reluctant Prophet

Now we come to one of the most famous and dramatic stories in the entire Bible: Jonah and the fish! The word of the Lord comes to Jonah son of Amittai: "Go to the great city of Nineveh and preach against it, because its wickedness has come up before me." But here's the huge problem: Nineveh is the capital of Assyria, Israel's brutal enemy. The Assyrians are known for their violence and cruelty. They're the people everyone fears. Jonah absolutely doesn't want them to repent and be forgiven. He'd rather see God destroy them completely! So Jonah makes a foolish decision—he decides to run away from God. He goes to the port city of Joppa, finds a ship heading to Tarshish (the complete opposite direction from Nineveh), pays the fare, and boards the ship, thinking, "I'll just get as far from Nineveh as possible." But you can't run from God! God sends a massive, violent storm. The wind howls. The waves crash over the boat. The ship is about to break apart. The experienced sailors are terrified—they've probably been through storms before, but nothing like this. They cry out to their gods and throw cargo overboard trying to lighten the ship. Meanwhile, Jonah? He's down below deck, fast asleep! The captain comes and wakes him: "How can you sleep? Get up and call on your god! Maybe he'll notice us and we won't die!" The sailors cast lots (like drawing straws) to find out whose fault this storm is, and the lot falls on Jonah. They bombard him with questions: "Who are you? Where are you from? What have you done?" Jonah confesses: "I'm a Hebrew, and I worship the Lord, the God of heaven, who made the sea and the dry land." Then he admits he's running from the Lord. The sailors are terrified—even more afraid now! "What should we do?" they ask. Jonah says, "Throw me into the sea, and it will become calm. I know it's my fault this storm has come on you." The sailors don't want to throw Jonah overboard, so they row harder trying to get back to land, but they can't. Finally, they reluctantly toss Jonah into the raging sea. Immediately, the storm stops. The sea becomes calm. And then—GULP!—God sends a huge fish that swallows Jonah whole. Jonah spends three days and three nights inside the fish's belly. Imagine that! It's dark, wet, smelly, and terrifying. But from inside the fish, Jonah prays to God. He realizes he can't escape God. He repents and thanks God for saving his life. God hears his prayer, and after three days, He commands the fish to vomit Jonah onto dry land. Jonah is spit out onto a beach, probably covered in fish slime! God gives Jonah a second chance: "Go to Nineveh." This time,

Jonah obeys. He proclaims, "Forty more days and Nineveh will be overthrown!" To Jonah's surprise (and annoyance), the people believe God's message. They fast, wear sackcloth, and repent. Even the king gets involved! When God sees their repentance, He has compassion and doesn't destroy the city. But Jonah is angry! He wanted Nineveh destroyed. God gently rebukes Jonah, teaching him about compassion. Fun Fact: Jesus later referred to Jonah—just as Jonah was in the fish for three days, Jesus would be in the tomb for three days before rising again! Jonah's story teaches us: You can't run from God. Wherever you go, God is there. God's mercy extends to everyone. Even people we don't like. God loves all people and wants everyone to repent. Obedience matters, even when it's hard. God wants willing, joyful obedience. God is patient with us. Jonah was stubborn, selfish, and angry. But God didn't give up on him. Think About It: - Jonah didn't want his enemies to be forgiven. Is there someone you're having trouble forgiving? What does Jonah's story teach us about forgiveness?

## Micah: Justice, Mercy, and Humility

Micah prophesied at the same time as Isaiah, speaking to both Northern and Southern Kingdoms. Like Amos, Micah's message focuses on justice. He calls out corrupt leaders, priests, and prophets who exploit the poor, take bribes, and twist justice. Micah prophesies that a ruler will come from Bethlehem who will shepherd God's people and bring peace. This is a prophecy about Jesus! Micah 5:2 says, "But you, Bethlehem Ephrathah, though you are small... out of you will come for me one who will be ruler over Israel." Hundreds of years later, Jesus was born in Bethlehem! One of the most famous verses in the Bible is Micah 6:8: "He has shown you, O mortal, what is good. And what does the Lord require of you? To act justly and to love mercy and to walk humbly with your God." Let's break that down: Act justly - Treat people fairly. Stand up for what's right. Love mercy - Show kindness and compassion. Forgive people. Walk humbly with your God - Don't be proud. Recognize that God is God, and you're not. Micah ends with a beautiful declaration: "Who is a God like you, who pardons sin and forgives the transgression... You do not stay angry forever but delight to show mercy" (Micah 7:18). What an amazing God we serve!

Activity Time: Create a "Micah 6:8 Reminder Card." Draw three sections: a scale for "Act Justly," a heart for "Love Mercy," and praying hands for "Walk Humbly with God." Decorate it and put it where you'll see it daily.

Pick one of the three to practice this week! For Parents: Discuss Micah 6:8 with your child. Ask: "What does it look like in our family to act justly (treat each other fairly), love mercy (forgive each other), and walk humbly with God (pray together)?" Make it practical and age-appropriate.

# Chapter 10: The Minor Prophets Part 2: Nahum through Malachi

# Chapter 10: The Minor Prophets Part 2 Think about the last page of a really good book—the kind that wraps up the story but leaves you eager for what comes next. That's what the final six prophets are like. They're bringing the Old Testament to a close while building anticipation for something amazing. These last prophets—Nahum, Habakkuk, Zephaniah, Haggai, Zechariah, and Malachi—remind God's people of His faithfulness and promise that the Messiah is coming!

## Nahum: God's Justice Against Nineveh

Remember Nineveh from Jonah? The city repented, and God spared them. That was about 100-150 years before Nahum. But now, Nineveh has gone back to its wicked ways. The Assyrians are brutal, cruel, and violent. They destroyed the Northern Kingdom. Nahum's message is short and powerful: God is going to judge Nineveh. This time, there's no call to repentance. Their time is up. Nahum describes God as "slow to anger" but also as someone who "will not leave the guilty unpunished" (Nahum 1:3). Nahum 1:7 gives a beautiful balance: "The Lord is good, a refuge in times of trouble. He cares for those who trust in him." God is a safe place for His people, but He's also a judge who will deal with evil. In 612 BC, Nineveh was completely destroyed. Evil doesn't get away with it forever. God sees, and He will bring justice. Fun Fact: Nineveh was so completely destroyed that for centuries, people thought it was just a myth—until archaeologists found its ruins in the 1800s!

## Habakkuk: Wrestling with Questions

Habakkuk is completely different from other prophets. Instead of God sending Habakkuk to deliver messages to the people, Habakkuk has an honest, raw conversation directly with God. He's asking the tough questions—the kind we all wonder about but sometimes feel we're not allowed to ask. Habakkuk looks around at Judah and sees violence, injustice, and sin everywhere. Wicked people are hurting the innocent. Courts are corrupt. Nobody seems to care about God's law. And God doesn't seem to be doing anything about it! So Habakkuk cries out in frustration, "How long, Lord, must I call for help, but you do not listen? Or cry out to you, 'Violence!' but you do not save?" (Habakkuk 1:2). He's essentially asking, "God, why don't you do something? Why are you letting this happen?" God's answer shocks Habakkuk: "Look at the nations and watch—and be utterly amazed. I am going to do something in your days that you would not believe, even if you were told. I am raising up the Babylonians, that ruthless and impetuous people." God is saying, "I AM doing something. I'm going to use the Babylonians to punish Judah for their sin." But wait! That creates an even bigger problem for Habakkuk. The Babylonians are even MORE wicked than Judah! They're brutal, violent, and worship false gods. They destroy entire nations. Habakkuk protests: "Your eyes are too pure to look on evil; you cannot tolerate wrongdoing. Why then do you tolerate the treacherous? Why are you silent while the wicked swallow up those more righteous than themselves?" (Habakkuk 1:13). He's asking, "How can You use evil people to punish people who are less evil? That doesn't seem fair!" God's answer is profound and important: Trust Me. I'm sovereign over everything. The Babylonians will get their punishment too—nobody escapes My justice. Even though it doesn't make sense now, I'm in control of history. Then God tells Habakkuk something incredibly important that becomes foundational to Christianity: "The righteous person will live by his faithfulness" (Habakkuk 2:4). This verse is quoted multiple times in the New Testament—in Romans, Galatians, and Hebrews. It means we're saved and we live by faith, trusting God even when we don't understand everything. We don't need all the answers—we need faith in the One who has all the answers. By the end, Habakkuk has come to trust. He says, "Though the fig tree does not bud and there are no grapes on the vines... yet I will rejoice in the Lord, I will be joyful in God my Savior" (Habakkuk 3:17-18). Even if everything goes wrong, I'll still trust God. Think About It: - Habakkuk brought his honest questions to God. What questions do you have for God? It's okay to ask Him!

## Zephaniah: The Day of the Lord

Zephaniah prophesies during King Josiah's reign. His message focuses on "the Day of the Lord"—a day of judgment when God will deal with sin. Zephaniah's description is intense. He calls it "a day of wrath, a day of distress and anguish" (Zephaniah 1:15). God will judge Judah for idolatry and surrounding nations for rejecting Him. But there's good news too. After judgment, God promises to restore a humble and faithful remnant. He says, "The Lord your God is with you, the Mighty Warrior who saves. He will take great delight in you; in his love he will no longer rebuke you, but will rejoice over you with singing" (Zephaniah 3:17). Can you imagine that? God rejoicing over you with singing! God doesn't just tolerate His people—He delights in them. Fun Fact: Zephaniah 3:17 says God "rejoices over you with singing"—God sings over His people with joy!

## Haggai: Get Back to Work!

After the exile, Jews returned to Jerusalem to rebuild the Temple. They started enthusiastically, but then got discouraged and gave up. They focused on building their own nice houses instead of God's house. Haggai's message is simple: "Get back to work!" He tells the people, "You're living in fancy houses while God's house remains in ruins?" He challenges them to think about their priorities. The people listen and start rebuilding. Haggai encourages them by saying that even though this Temple won't be as grand as Solomon's, God's presence will be there. And one day, God says, "I will fill this house with glory" (Haggai 2:7). This is a prophecy about Jesus, who would come to the Temple.

## Zechariah: Visions of Hope

Zechariah is Haggai's contemporary. While Haggai focuses on the immediate task, Zechariah gives the people a bigger vision of what God will do in the future. Zechariah's book is filled with eight visions! These are symbolic, communicating messages about God's judgment, purification, and restoration. But the most important parts are prophecies about the Messiah: Zechariah 9:9 - "Rejoice greatly, Daughter Zion! See, your king comes to you, righteous and victorious, lowly and riding on a donkey." This was fulfilled when Jesus rode into Jerusalem on Palm Sunday! Zechariah 11:12-13 - The Messiah will be betrayed for thirty pieces of silver. That's exactly what happened when Judas betrayed Jesus! Zechariah 12:10 - "They will look on me, the one they have pierced." This describes Jesus' crucifixion. Zechariah 13:1 - "A fountain will be opened... to cleanse them from sin." Jesus' blood cleanses us from sin! Zechariah also encourages the people to live righteously: "Administer true justice; show mercy and compassion" (Zechariah 7:9-10). God cares deeply about how we treat others. Think About It: - Zechariah prophesied hundreds of years before Jesus, but his prophecies came true exactly. What does this tell you about God's Word?

## Malachi: The Final Word

Malachi is the very last book of the Old Testament—the final prophet before centuries of silence. His name means "my messenger," fitting since he's delivering God's final message before the curtain closes on the Old Testament era. Malachi writes to people who have returned from exile in Babylon. The Temple has been rebuilt. They're back in the Promised Land. You'd think they'd be excited and grateful, right? But there's a major problem: their hearts aren't in it. They're just going through the motions of worship. Their relationship with God has become cold, routine, and halfhearted. They don't really love God anymore—they just show up because they're supposed to. What does this spiritual coldness look like? They're bringing sick, crippled, and diseased animals as sacrifices to God instead of their best. Imagine giving your friend your broken, used stuff instead of something good! The priests who are supposed to lead worship have become corrupt and lazy. They're teaching people incorrectly. Men are divorcing their wives for no good reason. People are withholding their tithes—keeping God's money for themselves. And worst of all, they're complaining and saying cynical things like, "What's the point of serving God? It doesn't make any difference." God confronts each issue directly through Malachi. The book is written like a debate or argument. God makes a statement, and the people argue back. God says, "I have loved you" (Malachi 1:2). But instead of responding with gratitude, the people cynically respond, "How have you loved us?" Their hearts have become hard, bitter, and ungrateful. They've forgotten everything God has done for them—bringing them back from exile, restoring Jerusalem, protecting them. One famous passage is about tithing. God says, "Bring the whole tithe into the storehouse... Test me in this... and see if I will not throw open the floodgates of heaven and pour out so much blessing" (Malachi 3:10). God invites the people to trust Him by giving generously. Then comes the final prophecy of the Old Testament. Malachi says, "See, I will send the prophet Elijah to you before that great and dreadful day of the Lord comes"

(Malachi 4:5). In the New Testament, we learn that John the Baptist came "in the spirit and power of Elijah." He prepared the way for Jesus! Fun Fact: After Malachi, there were 400 years of silence—no prophets, no new messages from God. Then an angel appeared to announce John the Baptist's birth, breaking the silence!

## The 400 Silent Years

After Malachi, God stops speaking through prophets for 400 years. That's a long time! During these "silent years," a lot happens: Persian Empire falls, Alexander the Great conquers, Greek Empire rises and falls, Roman Empire takes control. But God isn't absent—He's working behind the scenes, setting the stage for the most important event in history: the coming of Jesus! When the time is right, God breaks the silence. An angel appears to a priest and announces that his wife will have a baby—John the Baptist, who will prepare the way for Jesus. And then, Jesus is born in Bethlehem, just as the prophets predicted!

## What the Old Testament Has Taught Us

We've finished the entire Old Testament—all 39 books! Let's reflect: God is the Creator. He made the world and us. Sin is serious. Adam and Eve's sin broke the world. God is faithful. Even when His people failed, He never gave up. God has a rescue plan. From the beginning, God promised to send a Savior. God cares about justice, mercy, and humility. He wants His people to treat others well. God's love is relentless. He pursues us and redeems us. The Messiah is coming! Every prophecy, every story has been building to this moment!

Activity Time: Create a "400 Years of Silence" timeline. On a long piece of paper, draw a line with "Malachi" on one end and "Jesus is Born!" on the other. In between, write "400 years of waiting." This helps you visualize how long God's people waited—and how faithfully God kept His promise!

For Parents: Discuss with your child what it might have felt like to wait 400 years for the Messiah. Ask: "Have you ever waited a long time for something important? How did you feel?" Connect this to how God's timing is perfect, even when we have to wait.

# Chapter 11: The Gospels Part 1: Matthew and Mark - Meet Jesus!

The wait is over! For 39 books and thousands of years, God's people have been waiting for the Messiah. The prophets promised He would come. And now, He's finally here! His name is Jesus, and He's about to change everything. The New Testament begins with four books called the Gospels: Matthew, Mark, Luke, and John. "Gospel" means "good news," and these books tell the best news in the world—the story of Jesus' life, death, and resurrection. Each Gospel writer tells the story from a slightly different angle. Together, they give us a full, beautiful picture of who Jesus is and what He came to do. In this chapter, we'll explore the first two Gospels: Matthew and Mark. Get ready to meet Jesus—the Son of God, the promised Messiah, the Savior of the world!

## Why Four Gospels?

You might wonder, "Why four books that tell the same story? Wouldn't one be enough?" Here's the answer: Jesus is so amazing that it takes multiple perspectives to capture who He is. Imagine you went to an amusement park with three friends. Afterward, you each write about it. You might focus on roller coasters. Your friend might write about food. Another might talk about games. You all went to the same place, but noticed different things because of your unique perspectives. That's what the four Gospels are like. Matthew, Mark, Luke, and John all tell Jesus' story, but they emphasize different aspects of His life. When we read all four, we get a richer, deeper understanding of who Jesus is. Fun Fact: Matthew, Mark, Luke, and John were written within the lifetime of people who knew Jesus personally—eyewitness accounts!

## Matthew: Jesus the King

Matthew was one of Jesus' twelve disciples. Before following Jesus, he was a tax collector—a hated job. But when Jesus called Matthew to follow Him, Matthew left everything and became a devoted disciple. Matthew writes his Gospel primarily for a Jewish audience. He wants to show them that Jesus is the long-awaited Messiah, the promised King. That's why Matthew quotes the Old Testament more than any other Gospel writer. He's constantly saying, "See? Jesus fulfilled this prophecy!"

## Jesus' Birth

Matthew's Gospel begins with something that might seem boring at first—a genealogy, a long family tree. But wait! This family tree is actually showing us something incredible: Jesus is a direct descendant of Abraham (the father of God's people) and King David (Israel's greatest king). This is hugely important because God promised the Messiah would come from David's royal line. Matthew is proving Jesus has the right family credentials to be the Messiah! Then comes the amazing story. An angel named Gabriel appears to a young woman named Mary in the small town of Nazareth. Mary is probably a teenager, engaged to a carpenter named Joseph. The angel's greeting startles her: "Greetings, you who are highly favored! The Lord is with you." Mary is confused and afraid. What does this mean? The angel explains: "Do not be afraid, Mary; you have found favor with God. You will conceive and give birth to a son, and you are to call him Jesus. He will be great and will be called the Son of the Most High. The Lord God will give him the throne of his father David, and he will reign forever!" Mary asks the obvious question: "How will this be, since I am a virgin?" The angel answers, "The Holy Spirit will come on you, and the power of the Most High will overshadow you. So the holy one to be born will be called the Son of God." This baby will be conceived by the Holy Spirit—a miracle! Mary responds with incredible faith: "I am the Lord's servant. May your word to me be fulfilled." She trusts God completely, even though this will be hard to explain and people might not believe her. When Joseph finds out Mary is pregnant, he's heartbroken—they haven't been married yet! He plans to quietly break their engagement. But an angel appears to him in a dream: "Joseph son of David, do not be afraid to take Mary home as your wife, because what is conceived in her is from the Holy Spirit. She will give birth to a son, and you are to give him the name Jesus, because he will save his people from their sins." This fulfills Isaiah's prophecy from 700 years earlier about a virgin giving birth to Immanuel, which means "God with us." Caesar Augustus issues a decree requiring everyone to register in their hometown for a census. Joseph and Mary must travel from Nazareth to Bethlehem—a journey of about 80 miles—because Joseph is a descendant of David. And where is Bethlehem? It's the town the prophet

Micah said the Messiah would be born! God is orchestrating everything perfectly. Jesus is born in Bethlehem, just as Micah predicted 700 years earlier. Wise men—probably astrologers from Persia or Babylon—see a special star and follow it hundreds of miles to find the newborn King. They come to worship Him, bringing expensive gifts: gold (for a king), frankincense (for deity/worship), and myrrh (used for burial, foreshadowing His death). Even Gentiles from far away recognize Jesus as King!

## Jesus' Ministry Begins

When Jesus is about 30, He begins His public ministry. He's baptized by John the Baptist in the Jordan River. As Jesus comes up out of the water, the Holy Spirit descends like a dove, and God the Father speaks: "This is my Son, whom I love; with him I am well pleased." All three persons of the Trinity are present! Then Jesus is led into the wilderness, where He fasts for 40 days and is tempted by Satan. But Jesus resists every temptation by quoting Scripture. He shows us that God's Word is powerful and can help us fight temptation. Jesus begins teaching and performing miracles. He calls twelve disciples to follow Him—ordinary guys like fishermen and a tax collector.

## The Sermon on the Mount

One of the most famous sections is the Sermon on the Mount (chapters 5-7). Jesus sits on a mountainside and teaches about God's kingdom. He gives the Beatitudes: - "Blessed are the poor in spirit, for theirs is the kingdom of heaven." - "Blessed are those who mourn, for they will be comforted." - "Blessed are the merciful, for they will be shown mercy." Jesus teaches about anger, lust, revenge, and loving your enemies. He says, "Love your enemies and pray for those who persecute you." That's radical! He also teaches about prayer, giving, fasting, worry, and judging others. He says, "Seek first his kingdom and his righteousness, and all these things will be given to you as well."

## Miracles and Parables

Jesus performs countless miracles. He heals the sick, gives sight to the blind, makes the lame walk, casts out demons, calms storms, walks on water, and raises the dead. These miracles show that Jesus has power over sickness, nature, evil spirits, and death. He's not just a good teacher—He's God in the flesh! Jesus also teaches using parables—short stories with spiritual lessons. One important parable is the Sheep and the Goats. Jesus says, "Whatever you did for one of the least of these brothers and sisters of mine, you did for me." The way we treat others shows whether we truly love Jesus. Think About It: - Jesus said "Love your enemies and pray for those who persecute you." Who's hard for you to love? How can you pray for them this week?

## Peter's Confession

One day, Jesus asks His disciples, "Who do you say I am?" Peter answers, "You are the Messiah, the Son of the living God." Jesus is pleased. This is the central truth of the Gospel: Jesus is the Messiah, the Son of God. Everything hinges on this.

## Jesus' Death and Resurrection

As Jesus' ministry progresses and His popularity grows, the religious leaders—the Pharisees, Sadducees, and chief priests—become increasingly threatened. They see Jesus as a danger to their power and position. They start plotting how to kill Him. They need to do it during Passover when Jerusalem is crowded, but they need to be careful not to cause a riot. That's when one of Jesus' own disciples, Judas Iscariot, approaches them. "What are you willing to give me if I deliver him over to you?" Judas asks. They agree to pay him thirty pieces of silver (the price of a slave)—exactly fulfilling Zechariah's prophecy from 500 years earlier! Jesus knows what's coming. He gathers His twelve disciples for the Passover meal—what we now call the Last Supper. In an upper room, they recline around the table. During the meal, Jesus takes bread, gives thanks, breaks it, and gives it to His disciples saying, "Take and eat; this is my body." Then He takes a cup of wine, gives thanks, and says, "Drink from it, all of you. This is my blood of the covenant, which is poured out for many for the forgiveness of sins." He's explaining that His body will be broken and His blood will be shed—He's the ultimate Passover Lamb, sacrificed so we can be forgiven. After dinner, Jesus and His disciples go to the Garden of Gethsemane on the Mount of Olives. Jesus takes Peter, James, and John deeper into the garden with Him. He tells them, "My soul is overwhelmed with sorrow to the point of death. Stay here and keep watch with me." Then Jesus walks a bit farther and falls face-down on the ground. He's in agony, sweating drops of blood, struggling with what's about to happen. He prays, "My Father, if it is possible, may this cup be taken from me. Yet not as I will, but as you will." He's asking if there's any other way to save humanity besides the cross. But He knows there isn't. Three times He prays this prayer, surrendering completely to the Father's will. While Jesus is praying, His disciples keep falling asleep—they can't stay awake. Then suddenly, torches appear in the darkness. Judas arrives leading a large crowd of soldiers and officials armed with swords and clubs, sent by the chief priests. Judas walks up to Jesus and greets Him with a kiss—the prearranged signal identifying which man is Jesus. Jesus looks at him and says sadly, "Judas, are you betraying the Son of Man with a kiss?" Jesus is arrested. The disciples all flee in terror—they abandon Him. Jesus is dragged before the Sanhedrin (the Jewish ruling council) for a mock trial in the middle of the night. They bring false witnesses who contradict each other. Finally, the high priest asks Jesus directly: "Are you the Messiah, the Son of the Blessed One?" Jesus answers, "I am. And you will see the Son of Man sitting at the right hand of the Mighty One and coming on the clouds of heaven." The high priest tears his clothes and shouts, "Blasphemy! What more witnesses do we need?" They condemn Jesus to death. But the Jewish leaders don't have authority to execute anyone—only Rome can do that. So they take Jesus to Pontius Pilate, the Roman governor. Pilate questions Jesus but finds Him innocent. He tries to release Jesus, offering the crowd a choice: free Jesus or Barabbas (a rebel and murderer). But the chief priests have stirred up the crowd. They shout, "Crucify him! Crucify him!" Pilate asks, "Why? What crime has he committed?" But they shout even louder, "Crucify him!" Finally, Pilate gives in. He washes his hands symbolically and sentences an innocent man to death. Jesus is beaten, mocked, and forced to carry His cross to Golgotha. There, He's nailed to the cross between two criminals. Above His head is a sign: "This is Jesus, the King of the Jews." As Jesus hangs on the cross, darkness covers the land. Jesus cries out, "My God, my God, why have you forsaken me?" He's bearing the full weight of humanity's sin, experiencing separation from God the Father. Then Jesus says, "It is finished," and He dies. The curtain in the Temple—the one that separated people from God's presence—tears in two from top to bottom. The barrier between God and humanity is broken! Jesus' sacrifice has opened the way for us to have a relationship with God. Jesus' body is buried in a tomb. But on the third day, something incredible happens. An angel rolls away the stone, and Jesus rises from the dead! The tomb is empty. Jesus is alive! Jesus appears to His disciples and many others. He has a real, physical body. He's conquered death! And because He's alive, everyone who believes in Him can have eternal life. Jesus gives His disciples the Great Commission: "Go and make disciples of all nations, baptizing them in the name of the Father and of the Son and of the Holy Spirit, and teaching them to obey everything I have commanded you. And surely I am with you always, to the very end of the age." Fun Fact: The Great Commission (Matthew 28:19-20) is considered the mission statement for all Christians—to share the gospel with the world!

## Mark: Jesus the Servant

Mark's Gospel is the shortest and moves fast. Mark doesn't spend much time on Jesus' birth or teachings. He jumps right into the action, showing us what Jesus did. Mark's theme is Jesus the Servant—someone who came not to be served, but to serve and give His life as a ransom for many.

## Immediate Action

One of Mark's favorite words is "immediately." He uses it over 40 times! Everything happens quickly. Jesus is baptized, tempted, calling disciples, healing people, teaching, casting out demons—boom, boom, boom. Mark wants us to see Jesus as a man of action, always moving, always serving.

## Jesus the Miracle Worker

Mark highlights Jesus' miracles. He heals Peter's mother-in-law, cleanses a leper, heals a paralyzed man, calms a storm, casts demons into pigs, heals a bleeding woman, raises a dead girl, feeds 5,000 people with five loaves and two fish, and walks on water. The miracles keep coming! These aren't just cool displays of power. They show us who Jesus is. He has authority over sickness, nature, demons, and death. He's compassionate and cares about people's needs. And He's the Messiah prophesied in the Old Testament.

## Jesus Predicts His Death

As Jesus' ministry continues, He begins telling His disciples He's going to Jerusalem, where He'll suffer, die, and rise again. The disciples don't understand. Peter even rebukes Him! But Jesus says, "Get behind me, Satan! You do not have in mind the concerns of God, but merely human concerns." Jesus knows His death is part of God's plan—the only way to save humanity from sin. Jesus says, "Whoever wants to be my disciple must deny themselves and take up their cross and follow me." Following Jesus requires sacrifice. But it's worth it. Think About It: - Jesus came to serve, not to be served. What's one way you can serve someone this week?

## The Cross and the Resurrection

Like Matthew, Mark tells the story of Jesus' final week in Jerusalem. Jesus enters the city on a donkey while people shout, "Hosanna!" But within days, the same crowds will shout, "Crucify him!" Jesus is betrayed, arrested, tried, mocked, beaten, and crucified. Mark emphasizes how Jesus suffered. He was treated like a criminal, even though He was innocent. He experienced physical pain, emotional anguish, and spiritual separation from the Father. He did all of this for us. But death couldn't hold Him! On the third day, Jesus rises from the dead. An angel tells the women, "He has risen! He is not here." Jesus appears to His disciples and commissions them to go into all the world and preach the gospel. Think About It: - Jesus rose from the dead! How does knowing Jesus is alive change the way you face hard situations?

## What We Learn from Matthew and Mark

Jesus is the promised Messiah. Everything the prophets said came true. He's the King the world has been waiting for. Jesus is both God and man. He performed miracles and rose from the dead—things only God can do. But He also got hungry, tired, and experienced human emotions. Jesus came to serve and save. He gave His life as a ransom for many. His death paid the price for our sins. Jesus' resurrection changes everything. Because Jesus rose from the dead, we can have eternal life. Death is not the end! Following Jesus requires commitment. He calls us to deny ourselves, take up our

cross, and follow Him. We're called to share the good news. Jesus commanded us to go and make disciples of all nations.
Activity Time: Create a "Jesus Timeline." Draw a line with key events from Jesus' life: Birth in Bethlehem → Baptism → Miracles → Last Supper → Crucifixion → Resurrection → Great Commission. Add drawings for each event. This helps you see the full story of Jesus' life! For Parents: Read the Great Commission (Matthew 28:19-20) together. Discuss: "How can our family 'make disciples'?" It might be inviting friends to church, showing kindness to neighbors, or praying for people who don't know Jesus. Make it practical and age-appropriate.

# Chapter 12: The Gospels Part 2: Luke and John - Jesus for Everyone!

Have you ever felt like you didn't fit in? Maybe you weren't popular enough, smart enough, or athletic enough. Maybe people looked down on you or left you out. If you've ever felt that way, you're going to love the Gospel of Luke. Luke shows us that Jesus came for everyone—not just the religious people or the popular crowd. Jesus welcomed outcasts, ate with sinners, and showed love to people everyone else ignored. No one is too broken, too poor, or too sinful for Jesus! And if you've ever wondered who Jesus really is, you're going to love the Gospel of John. John makes it clear: Jesus is God. He's the Light of the World, the Bread of Life, the Good Shepherd, and the Way to the Father. John shows us that Jesus isn't just a great teacher—He's the Son of God who came to give us eternal life.

## Luke: Jesus the Savior of All People

Luke was a doctor and a close companion of the apostle Paul. He wasn't one of the twelve disciples, but he carefully researched Jesus' life by talking to eyewitnesses. Luke writes his Gospel for a Gentile (non-Jewish) audience, and his main message is: Jesus came to save all people, no matter who they are.

## The Birth Stories

Luke gives us the most detailed account of Jesus' birth. He tells us about Zechariah and Elizabeth, an elderly couple who couldn't have children. An angel tells Zechariah they're going to have a son—John the Baptist, who will prepare the way for Jesus. Then the angel Gabriel appears to Mary and tells her she's going to give birth to the Son of God. Mary responds with faith: "I am the Lord's servant. May your word to me be fulfilled." When Jesus is born in Bethlehem, angels appear to shepherds in the fields. Shepherds were considered lowly, unimportant people. But God chose them to be the first to hear the good news! The angels say, "Today in the town of David a Savior has been born to you; he is the Messiah, the Lord." Luke is already showing us his theme: Jesus came for everyone, including the lowly and forgotten. Fun Fact: Luke includes more details about Mary than any other Gospel—he probably interviewed her directly to get the story!

## Jesus' Compassion for Outcasts

Throughout Luke's Gospel, we see Jesus reaching out to people society rejected. He touches lepers. He eats with tax collectors and sinners. He heals a bleeding woman. He raises a widow's son. He welcomes little children. He forgives a woman caught in adultery. He saves a criminal dying on the cross next to Him. The religious leaders criticize Jesus for spending time with "sinners." But Jesus says, "It is not the healthy who need a doctor, but the sick. I have not come to call the righteous, but sinners to repentance." Jesus came to seek and save the lost! Think About It: - Jesus welcomed people everyone else rejected. Is there someone at school or in your neighborhood who feels left out? How can you show them kindness this week?

## The Parables in Luke

Luke includes some of Jesus' most famous parables: The Good Samaritan (Luke 10) - A Jewish man is beaten by robbers and left on the road. A priest and Levite pass by. But a Samaritan—someone Jews normally hated—stops and takes care of him. Jesus asks, "Which was a neighbor?" The answer: the one who showed mercy. Jesus teaches us to love everyone, even people who are different from us. The Lost Sheep, Coin, and Son (Luke 15) - These three parables are all about what's lost being found! A shepherd has a hundred sheep, but one wanders off and gets lost. Does he say, "Oh well, I still have ninety-nine"? No! He leaves the ninety-nine in a safe place and goes searching for the one that's lost. When he finds it, he joyfully puts it on his shoulders and carries it home. He calls his friends together and says, "Rejoice with me; I have found my lost sheep!" Jesus says, "In the same way there will be more rejoicing in heaven over one sinner who repents than over ninety-nine righteous persons who do not need to repent." God doesn't give up on anyone! A woman has ten silver coins, but she loses one. Does she shrug it off? No! She lights a lamp, sweeps the entire house carefully, and searches until she finds it. When she does, she calls her friends and neighbors together and says, "Rejoice with me; I have found my lost coin!" Again, Jesus says there's rejoicing in heaven over one sinner who repents. The Parable of the Lost Son (Prodigal Son) is especially powerful and personal. A man has two sons. The younger son comes to his father and says something incredibly disrespectful: "Father, give me my share of the estate." He's basically saying, "I wish you were dead so I could have your money." But the father divides his property and gives the son what he asks for. The younger son takes the money and leaves home. He travels to a distant country where nobody knows him and wastes everything on wild, reckless living—partying, drinking, and foolish spending. Eventually, the money runs out completely. And to make matters worse, a severe famine hits the region. The son is desperate and starving. He takes a job feeding pigs—the most humiliating job a Jewish person could have! He's so hungry that he longs to eat the pods that the pigs are eating. He's hit rock bottom. Finally, he comes to his senses. He thinks, "How many of my father's hired servants have food to spare, and here I am starving to death! I will set out and go back to my father and say to him: Father, I have sinned against heaven and against you. I am no longer worthy to be called your son; make me like one of your hired servants." So he starts the long journey home, rehearsing his apology speech. But here's the incredible part: "While he was still a long way off, his father saw him and was filled with compassion for him." The father had been watching and waiting! He runs to his son—which would have been undignified for a wealthy man, but he doesn't care—he throws his arms around him and kisses him. The son starts his speech: "Father, I have sinned against heaven and against you. I am no longer worthy to be called your son." But the father interrupts him! He calls to his servants: "Quick! Bring the best robe and put it on him. Put a ring on his finger and sandals on his feet. Bring the fattened calf and kill it. Let's have a feast and celebrate!" The father throws a huge party because "this son of mine was dead and is alive again; he was lost and is found!" That's exactly how God feels when we come back to Him after wandering away! He doesn't scold us or make us grovel. He runs to us with open arms! He celebrates! He restores us completely! The Pharisee and the Tax Collector (Luke 18) - A Pharisee prays, "God, I thank you that I'm not like other people." But the tax collector prays, "God, have mercy on me, a sinner." Jesus says the tax collector went home justified before God. Why? Because God opposes the proud but gives grace to the humble. Fun Fact: The Parable of the Prodigal Son is only found in Luke—it's one of the most beloved stories in the entire Bible!

## Jesus' Final Week and Resurrection

Like the other Gospels, Luke tells the story of Jesus' final week. But Luke includes unique details. On the cross, Jesus says, "Father, forgive them, for they do not know what they are doing." Even while suffering, Jesus shows mercy! One of the criminals hanging next to Jesus says, "Jesus, remember me when you come into your kingdom." Jesus replies, "Truly I tell you, today you will be with me in paradise." It's never too late to turn to Jesus! After Jesus rises, He appears to two disciples on the road to Emmaus. They don't recognize Him at first. Jesus explains how all the Scriptures point to Him. When they finally realize it's Jesus, He disappears. Luke ends with Jesus ascending to heaven. He blesses His disciples and is taken up. The disciples return to Jerusalem with great joy, praising God. Think About It: - The criminal on the cross turned to Jesus at the last moment and was saved. What does this tell you about God's mercy?

## John: Jesus the Son of God

John's Gospel is different from Matthew, Mark, and Luke. John doesn't focus as much on parables or miracles. Instead, John focuses on who Jesus is and what He came to do. John makes it clear from the very first verse: Jesus is God.

## In the Beginning Was the Word

John's Gospel starts with beautiful, profound words: "In the beginning was the Word, and the Word was with God, and the Word was God. He was with God in the beginning. Through him all things were made." Who is "the Word"? It's Jesus! John is saying that Jesus has always existed. He was there at creation. He is God. And then John says, "The Word became flesh and made his dwelling among us" (John 1:14). Jesus, who is God, became a human being and lived among us!

## The "I Am" Statements

Throughout John's Gospel, Jesus makes seven powerful "I am" statements. When Jesus says "I am," He's identifying Himself as God! Here are the seven: 1. "I am the bread of life" (John 6:35) - Jesus satisfies our spiritual hunger. 2. "I am the light of the world" (John 8:12) - Jesus brings truth and guidance. 3. "I am the door" (John 10:9) - Jesus is the way to salvation. 4. "I am the good shepherd" (John 10:11) - Jesus cares for and protects us. 5. "I am the resurrection and the life" (John 11:25) - Jesus has power over death. 6. "I am the way and the truth and the life" (John 14:6) - Jesus is the only way to God. 7. "I am the vine" (John 15:5) - Jesus is the source of our spiritual life. These statements show us that Jesus is everything we need!

## John 3:16 - The Heart of the Gospel

One of the most famous verses in the Bible is John 3:16: "For God so loved the world that he gave his one and only Son, that whoever believes in him shall not perish but have eternal life." This verse sums up the gospel: - God loves the world - God's love is for everyone, everywhere. - He gave His Son - God gave Jesus to die for us. - Whoever believes in Him - Salvation is available to anyone who believes. - Shall not perish but have eternal life - We can have a forever relationship with God! Fun Fact: John 3:16 is called "the gospel in a nutshell" because it summarizes the entire message of salvation in one verse!

## Jesus' Miracles in John

John carefully selects and records seven key miracles—he calls them "signs" because they're not just displays of power, they're signs pointing to who Jesus is: 1. Turning water into wine (John 2) - Jesus' first miracle at a wedding in Cana. He turns 180 gallons of water into the finest wine! This shows His power over creation itself. 2. Healing an official's son (John 4) - A royal official's son is dying. Jesus heals him from a distance—without even being in the same town! This shows His power over space. 3. Healing a paralyzed man (John 5) - A man had been paralyzed for thirty-eight years. Jesus heals him instantly! This shows His power over time and chronic conditions. 4. Feeding 5,000 people (John 6) - Jesus takes a boy's five loaves and two fish and multiplies them to feed a massive crowd. This proves He's the Bread of Life—the one who truly satisfies. 5. Walking on water (John 6) - Jesus walks on the stormy Sea of Galilee to reach His frightened disciples. This shows His power over nature itself. 6. Healing a blind man (John 9) - Jesus heals a man born blind, giving him sight for the first time in his life. This proves Jesus is the Light of the World—He opens our spiritual eyes. 7. Raising Lazarus from the dead (John 11) - Lazarus has been dead and buried for four days. Jesus calls, "Lazarus, come out!" and he walks out of the tomb, still wrapped in grave clothes! This ultimate miracle proves Jesus is the Resurrection and the Life—He has complete power over death itself. Each carefully chosen miracle points to a specific aspect of Jesus' identity and power. Together they demonstrate that He's not just a good man or a wise teacher—He's God in human flesh!

## The Crucifixion and Resurrection

John's account of the crucifixion emphasizes Jesus' control and purpose. From the cross, He makes sure His mother Mary is cared for. He says, "I am thirsty" (fulfilling prophecy), and then, "It is finished." His mission is complete. When Jesus rises, He appears to Mary Magdalene first. Then to the disciples. But Thomas isn't there. When the others tell him, "We have seen the Lord!" Thomas says, "Unless I see the nail marks, I will not believe." A week later, Jesus appears again. He tells Thomas, "Put your finger here; see my hands. Stop doubting and believe." Thomas responds, "My Lord and my God!" Jesus says, "Because you have seen me, you have believed; blessed are those who have not seen and yet have believed." That's us! We haven't seen Jesus with our eyes, but we believe. And Jesus says we're blessed! John ends by saying he wrote his Gospel "that you may believe that Jesus is the Messiah, the Son of God, and that by believing you may have life in his name" (John 20:31). Think About It: - John says those who believe without seeing are blessed. What helps you believe in Jesus even though you can't see Him?

## What We Learn from Luke and John

Jesus came for everyone. Rich or poor, Jew or Gentile, sinner or saint—Jesus welcomes all who come to Him. Jesus is compassionate. He sees the hurting, the lonely, the rejected, and He reaches out with love. Jesus is God. John makes this crystal clear. Jesus is the Son of God, equal with the Father. Salvation is a gift. We receive it by believing in Jesus. John 3:16 tells us that whoever believes will have eternal life. We're called to love and serve. Just like Jesus served others humbly, we're called to do the same. The resurrection is central. Jesus didn't just die—He rose again! Because He's alive, we can have hope and eternal life.

Activity Time: Memorize John 3:16! Write it on a card and decorate it with hearts (God's love), a cross (Jesus' death), and a sunrise (eternal life). Put it where you'll see it every day. Try to memorize it by the end of the week! For Parents: Discuss the Parable of the Prodigal Son with your child. Ask: "How does the father in the story show us what God is like?" Talk about a time when your child made a mistake and you forgave them. Connect this to how God always welcomes us back with open arms when we turn to Him.

# Chapter 13: The Church Begins: Acts of the Apostles

Picture this: 120 believers are gathered in an upstairs room in Jerusalem, praying and waiting. Jesus has ascended to heaven and told them to wait for the gift He promised—the Holy Spirit. Suddenly, a sound like a violent wind fills the house. Tongues of fire appear and rest on each person. They begin speaking in languages they've never learned! People from all over the world hear them declaring God's wonders in their own languages. It's Pentecost, and the church is being born! The book of Acts is like an action movie—filled with miracles, bold preaching, dramatic rescues, shipwrecks, and the unstoppable spread of the gospel. Acts is the sequel to the Gospel of Luke, written by the same author. It tells how Jesus' followers took the good news from Jerusalem to the ends of the earth. Let's dive in!

## The Promise of the Holy Spirit

After Jesus rose from the dead, He spent 40 days teaching His disciples. Then, before He ascended to heaven, He told them, "Wait for the gift my Father promised... You will receive power when the Holy Spirit comes on you; and you will be my witnesses in Jerusalem, and in all Judea and Samaria, and to the ends of the earth" (Acts 1:4, 8). This verse is like a roadmap for Acts. The gospel will spread from Jerusalem to Judea and Samaria and eventually to the ends of the earth. That's exactly what happens! Then Jesus is taken up to heaven before their eyes. Two angels appear and say, "This same Jesus, who has been taken from you into heaven, will come back in the same way" (Acts 1:11). Jesus will return one day! Fun Fact: The book of Acts covers about 30 years of early church history—from Jesus' ascension (around 30 AD) to Paul in Rome (around 62 AD)!

## Pentecost: The Holy Spirit Comes

Ten days after Jesus ascends to heaven, the Day of Pentecost arrives. This is an important Jewish festival celebrating the wheat harvest, and Jerusalem is packed with Jewish pilgrims from all over the known world—Parthia, Media, Elam, Mesopotamia, Egypt, Rome, Crete, Arabia, and many other places. They've traveled hundreds or thousands of miles to celebrate in Jerusalem. Meanwhile, about 120 believers—Jesus' apostles, His mother Mary, other women, and His brothers—are gathered together in an upstairs room, praying and waiting for what Jesus promised. Suddenly, at about nine o'clock in the morning, something extraordinary happens! There's a sound like a violent, rushing wind that fills the entire house where they're sitting. What looks like tongues of fire appear and rest on each person. And they're all filled with the Holy Spirit! They begin speaking in languages they've never learned—real human languages from all over the world. The commotion is so loud that it draws a crowd outside. Jews from every nation hear these Galileans speaking in their own native languages! Parthians hear Parthian. Egyptians hear Egyptian. Romans hear Latin. Everyone hears them declaring the wonderful works of God in languages they understand perfectly. They're utterly amazed and perplexed, asking one another, "What does this mean?" But some skeptics in the crowd mock, sneering, "They've had too much wine!" That's when Peter stands up boldly (remember, this is the same Peter who denied Jesus three times just weeks ago!). He raises his voice and addresses the crowd: "Fellow Jews and all of you who live in Jerusalem, let me explain this to you! These people are not drunk, as you suppose—it's only nine in the morning! No, this is what was spoken by the prophet Joel: 'In the last days, God says, I will pour out my Spirit on all people.'" Then Peter preaches one of the most powerful sermons ever delivered. He tells them about Jesus—His miracles, His crucifixion, and His resurrection. He quotes Psalm 16 and Psalm 110, proving from Scripture that the Messiah had to die and rise again. Then Peter boldly declares: "God has made this Jesus, whom you crucified, both Lord and Messiah!" The crowd is cut to the heart—they feel convicted, troubled, desperate. They cry out, "Brothers, what shall we do?" Peter doesn't hesitate: "Repent and be baptized, every one of you, in the name of Jesus Christ for the forgiveness of your sins. And you will receive the gift of the Holy Spirit. The promise is for you and your children and for all who are far off—for all whom the Lord our God will call." That very day, about 3,000 people believe Peter's message and are baptized! The church explodes from 120 believers to over 3,120 in a single day! The Holy Spirit has come, and nothing will ever be the same! Think About It: - The disciples waited for God's timing before the Holy Spirit came. When have you had to wait for God's timing?

## The Early Church

The new believers devote themselves to the apostles' teaching, fellowship, breaking bread (communion), and prayer. They share everything they have, selling property to help anyone in need. They meet together praising God. And the Lord adds to their number daily! The early church is united, generous, and full of joy. They experience miracles too. Peter and John heal a man lame from birth. The man jumps up, walks, and praises God. When people gather in amazement, Peter preaches, and 5,000 more people believe! But not everyone is happy. The religious leaders arrest Peter and John and command them to stop preaching. Peter boldly responds, "We cannot help speaking about what we have seen and heard!"

## Stephen: The First Martyr

A man named Stephen is full of faith, the Holy Spirit, wisdom, and power. He performs miracles and speaks boldly about Jesus. But some oppose him and bring false charges. He's brought before the high council. Stephen gives a powerful speech, recounting Israel's history and pointing out how people have always resisted God's messengers. He says, "You always resist the Holy Spirit! You killed the prophets who predicted the Righteous One, and now you've betrayed and murdered Him!" The leaders are enraged. But Stephen, full of the Holy Spirit, looks up and sees heaven opened and Jesus standing at God's right hand. He says, "Look, I see heaven open and the Son of Man standing at the right hand of God!" They rush at him, drag him out of the city, and stone him to death. As they're stoning him, Stephen prays, "Lord Jesus, receive my spirit... Lord, do not hold this sin against them." Then he dies. Stephen becomes the first Christian martyr. Watching this execution is a young man named Saul, who approves. But Saul's story is about to change! Fun Fact: Stephen's prayer "do not hold this sin against them" echoes Jesus' words on the cross: "Father, forgive them"!

## Saul's Conversion

Meanwhile, a young man named Saul is causing absolute terror among Jesus' followers. He's a Pharisee, zealous for Jewish law, and he's convinced that this new "Jesus movement" is dangerous blasphemy that must be stopped. He's "breathing out murderous threats" against believers, going from house to house in Jerusalem, dragging men and women off to prison. Many believers have fled Jerusalem because of him. But Saul isn't satisfied. He goes to the high priest and asks for official letters to the synagogues in Damascus (about 150 miles away), requesting permission to arrest any believers there—men or women—and bring them back to Jerusalem in chains. The high priest agrees, and Saul sets off on the road to Damascus with a group of men, determined to stamp out Christianity. But on the way to Damascus, around noon when the sun is at its brightest, something absolutely incredible happens. Suddenly, a light from heaven—brighter even than the noonday sun—flashes around Saul! He falls to the ground, completely overwhelmed. Then he hears a voice speaking to him: "Saul, Saul, why do you persecute me?" The voice is gentle but powerful. Saul, trembling and terrified, asks, "Who are you, Lord?" The answer shocks him to his core: "I am Jesus, whom you are persecuting. Now get up and go into the city, and you will be told what you must do." The men traveling with Saul stand there speechless—they hear the sound but don't see anyone. When Saul gets up from the ground and opens his eyes, he can't see anything! He's completely blind! His companions have to take his hand and lead him into Damascus like a little child. For three days, Saul sits in Damascus—blind, not eating, not drinking, thinking about everything that's happened. His whole world has been turned upside down. Jesus is alive! Meanwhile, the Lord speaks in a vision to a believer in Damascus named Ananias: "Go to the house of Judas on Straight Street and ask for a man from Tarsus named Saul, for he is praying. In a vision he has seen a man named Ananias come and place his hands on him to restore his sight." Ananias is terrified! He protests, "Lord, I have heard many reports about this man and all the harm he has done to your holy people in Jerusalem. And he has come here with authority from the chief priests to arrest all who call on your name!" But the Lord tells Ananias something amazing: "Go! This man is my chosen instrument to proclaim my name to the Gentiles and their kings and to the people of Israel. I will show him how much he must suffer for my name." So Ananias obeys—imagine his courage! He goes to the house, places his hands on Saul, and says, "Brother Saul, the Lord—Jesus, who appeared to you on the road as you were coming here—has sent me so that you may see again and be filled with the Holy Spirit." Immediately, something like scales falls from Saul's eyes, and he can see again! He gets up and is baptized, and he eats and regains his strength. Then Saul does something that shocks everyone: he immediately begins preaching in the synagogues that Jesus is the Son of God! The people who hear him are astonished. They ask, "Isn't he the man who raised havoc in Jerusalem among those who call on this name? And hasn't he come here to take them as prisoners to the chief priests?" But Saul grows more and more powerful, proving that Jesus is the Messiah. Saul (who later goes by his Roman name, Paul) becomes one of the church's greatest leaders, writing at least 13 books of the New Testament! God took Christianity's fiercest enemy and transformed him into its most effective missionary! Think About It: - God changed Saul from a persecutor to a preacher. Who in your life seems far from God? How can you pray for them?

## Peter's Vision and Cornelius

God gives Peter a vision to teach him that the gospel isn't just for Jews—it's for Gentiles (non-Jews) too! Peter sees a sheet coming down from heaven filled with "unclean" animals. A voice tells Peter, "Get up, kill and eat." But Peter refuses. The voice replies, "Do not call anything impure that God has made clean." Right after the vision, messengers arrive from a Roman centurion named Cornelius. Cornelius isn't Jewish, but he fears God. An angel has told him to send for Peter. Peter goes to Cornelius's house and shares the gospel. While Peter is speaking, the Holy Spirit falls on everyone listening! Peter realizes that God accepts people from every nation. Cornelius and his household are baptized, and the gospel begins spreading to Gentiles.

## Paul's Missionary Journeys

The rest of Acts focuses on Paul and his missionary journeys. Paul travels thousands of miles, planting churches and preaching about Jesus. Paul's journeys take him to Cyprus, Turkey, Macedonia, and Greece. He plants churches in Philippi, Thessalonica, Athens, and Corinth. In Philippi, Paul and Silas are thrown in prison. At midnight, they're praying and singing when an earthquake shakes the prison. All the doors fly open! The jailer is about to kill himself, but Paul stops him. That night, the jailer and his whole family believe and are baptized! Throughout his journeys, Paul faces incredible hardships—beatings, imprisonment, shipwrecks, and threats. But he never gives up. He's driven by his love for Jesus and his passion to see people saved. Fun Fact: Paul traveled over 10,000 miles during his missionary journeys—mostly on foot or by boat!

## Paul in Jerusalem and Rome

At the end of his third journey, Paul feels compelled to go to Jerusalem, even though warned that trouble awaits. Sure enough, when Paul arrives, a riot breaks out. The crowd tries to kill him, but Roman soldiers rescue him. Paul is arrested and spends two years in prison in Caesarea. Finally, Paul appeals to Caesar and is sent to Rome to stand trial. On the way to Rome, Paul's ship encounters a violent storm and is wrecked. But God protects everyone—all 276 people make it safely to land! They end up on the island of Malta, where Paul is bitten by a poisonous snake but suffers no harm. Paul heals many people and preaches the gospel. Finally, Paul reaches Rome. Acts ends with Paul under house arrest but still boldly preaching about Jesus. For two whole years, he welcomes all who come and teaches about God's kingdom. Nothing can stop the gospel! Think About It: - Paul faced shipwrecks, snakebites, and imprisonment but never stopped sharing Jesus. What obstacles make it hard for you to talk about your faith?

## What We Learn from Acts

The Holy Spirit empowers believers. The same Spirit who came at Pentecost lives in every Christian today. The church is unstoppable. Despite persecution, the gospel spread rapidly. When people try to stop God's work, it only spreads further! Courage comes from faith. Peter, who once denied Jesus, now boldly preaches. When you know Jesus, you can face anything with courage. God can change anyone. Saul went from persecutor to apostle. No one is too far gone! The gospel is for everyone. Salvation is for all people, not just one group. Suffering for Jesus is an honor. The apostles rejoiced when they suffered for Jesus' name. Prayer is powerful. Throughout Acts, believers pray, and God acts.

Activity Time: Create a "Missionary Journey Map." Draw a simple map showing Paul's travels from Jerusalem to Rome. Mark key cities: Antioch, Ephesus, Philippi, Athens, Corinth, and Rome. Label one event that happened in each city. This helps you visualize how far the gospel spread! For Parents: Discuss with your child how the early church "devoted themselves to the apostles' teaching, fellowship, breaking bread, and prayer"

(Acts 2:42). Ask: "How can our family practice these four things?" Make a plan to read the Bible together, spend time with Christian friends, take communion at church, and pray as a family.

# Chapter 14: Paul's Letters Part 1: Romans through Ephesians

Imagine getting a personal letter from your favorite teacher or mentor—someone who really cares about you and wants to help you grow. That's what Paul's letters are like. After Paul planted churches during his missionary journeys, he wrote letters to encourage them, answer their questions, correct their mistakes, and teach them more about Jesus. Paul wrote 13 letters included in the New Testament. In this chapter, we'll look at the first five: Romans, 1 Corinthians, 2 Corinthians, Galatians, and Ephesians. Each one has important lessons for us today!

## Romans: The Gospel Explained

Romans is Paul's longest and most theological letter—his masterpiece. He writes to the church in Rome, a church he didn't personally start but desperately hopes to visit someday. Paul has heard about their faith and wants to encourage them and teach them more. Romans isn't addressing specific problems like his other letters. Instead, it's like a systematic, detailed explanation of the entire gospel—what it is, why we desperately need it, and exactly how it works. If you want to understand Christianity, Romans is essential!

## Everyone Has Sinned

Paul starts by building his case carefully, like a lawyer presenting evidence. First, he makes a sobering point that everyone needs to understand: every single person has sinned. It doesn't matter if you're Jewish (with God's law) or Gentile (without God's law). It doesn't matter if you're religious or not, rich or poor, good or bad by human standards. Romans 3:23 delivers the verdict: "For all have sinned and fall short of the glory of God." ALL means ALL. That includes you, me, your parents, your teachers—everyone! Think about it this way: God's standard is perfection—His glory. And we've all fallen short. It's like trying to jump from California to Hawaii. Some people might jump farther than others, but nobody can jump thousands of miles across the ocean! We all fall short. And sin has serious consequences. Romans 6:23 explains: "The wages of sin is death." When you work, you earn wages—payment for what you've done. Sin "pays" death—spiritual separation from God, both now and eternally. That's terrifying news!

## But God Offers a Gift

But wait—Romans 6:23 doesn't stop there! The whole verse says, "The wages of sin is death, BUT the gift of God is eternal life in Christ Jesus our Lord." This is the incredible news! While sin pays wages we've earned, God offers something completely different—a GIFT! We don't earn salvation through being good enough or following rules. It's a gift, freely given! Romans 5:8 shows us why this is so amazing: "But God demonstrates his own love for us in this: While we were still sinners, Christ died for us." God didn't wait for us to clean ourselves up first. He didn't wait for us to get our act together. While we were still sinners—still rebellious, still falling short—Christ died for us! That's incredible love! So how do we receive this free gift? Not by working harder or being better. Through faith—trusting in what Jesus has done. Romans 10:9 explains: "If you declare with your mouth, 'Jesus is Lord,' and believe in your heart that God raised him from the dead, you will be saved." Confess Jesus as Lord. Believe He rose from death. Trust Him. That's it! Fun Fact: Romans 8 is one of the most encouraging chapters in the Bible—it talks about God's unstoppable love and promises that nothing can separate us from it!

## Life in the Spirit

Romans 8:1 says, "Therefore, there is now no condemnation for those who are in Christ Jesus." If you're in Christ, you're not condemned—you're forgiven! And Romans 8:28 promises, "In all things God works for the good of those who love him." The second half of Romans is about how to live out the gospel. Romans 12:2 says, "Do not conform to the pattern of this world, but be transformed by the renewing of your mind." Following Jesus changes how we think and live. Think About It: - Romans 8:28 says God works all things for good. Can you think of a hard situation that God used for good?

## 1 Corinthians: Dealing with Church Problems

The church in Corinth had big problems—divisions, sexual immorality, lawsuits between believers, confusion about spiritual gifts, and disorder in worship. Paul writes to address these issues and teach the church how to function properly.

## Unity in the Church

Paul addresses divisions. Some were saying, "I follow Paul!" Others, "I follow Apollos!" Paul says, "Is Christ divided? Were you baptized in the name of Paul?" He reminds them they're all one in Christ. Divisions hurt the church.

## Love Is the Greatest

One of the most famous chapters in the entire Bible is 1 Corinthians 13—the "love chapter." Paul has just been talking about spiritual gifts, and now he shows them "the most excellent way." He writes, "If I speak in the tongues of men or of angels, but do not have love, I am only a resounding gong or a clanging cymbal." Imagine someone banging on pots and pans—just noise! That's what even the most impressive spiritual gifts are without love. Love is more important than any spiritual gift, no matter how spectacular! Then Paul gives us one of the most beautiful descriptions of love ever written: "Love is patient, love is kind. It does not envy, it does not boast, it is not proud. It does not dishonor others, it is not self-seeking, it is not easily angered, it keeps no record of wrongs. Love does not delight in evil but rejoices with the truth. It always protects, always trusts, always hopes, always perseveres." Read that list slowly. That's real love—not the shallow, feeling-based love our culture talks about, but sacrificial, action-based, others-focused love. This is the kind of love Jesus showed us on the cross. This is the kind of love we're called to show others. And honestly, it's impossible in our own strength! We need God's help to love like this. Paul concludes: "And now these three remain: faith, hope and love. But the greatest of these is love." Without love, everything else is meaningless. Fun Fact: 1 Corinthians 13 is often read at weddings because it beautifully describes what true love looks like!

## The Resurrection Matters

In chapter 15, Paul defends the resurrection. Some were saying there's no resurrection. But Paul says if Christ wasn't raised, our faith is useless! The resurrection is essential. Because Jesus rose, we will rise too. Paul also talks about spiritual gifts. Every believer has gifts given by the Holy Spirit. We're all part of one body (the church), and every part is important. Use your gifts to build up the church!

## 2 Corinthians: Ministry and Suffering

Paul's second letter is more personal. He defends his ministry, encourages the church, and talks openly about his struggles.

## Comfort in Suffering

Paul says God "comforts us in all our troubles, so that we can comfort those in any trouble with the comfort we ourselves receive from God" (2 Corinthians 1:4). When you go through hard times, God comforts you. And then you can comfort others!

## A New Creation

One of the most famous verses is 2 Corinthians 5:17: "Therefore, if anyone is in Christ, the new creation has come: The old has gone, the new is here!" When you become a Christian, you're a new creation!

## Paul's Thorn

Paul mentions a "thorn in the flesh"—some kind of struggle or weakness. Paul prayed for God to remove it, but God said, "My grace is sufficient for you, for my power is made perfect in weakness" (2 Corinthians 12:9). Sometimes God doesn't remove our struggles, but He gives us grace to endure. And through our weaknesses, His power is displayed! Think About It: - Paul's weakness allowed God's power to shine. How might God use your weaknesses to show His strength?

## Galatians: Freedom in Christ

The Galatian churches were being influenced by false teachers who said you had to follow Jewish laws to be saved. Paul is upset and writes a strong letter to correct them.

## Justified by Faith, Not Works

Paul's main message: you're saved by faith in Jesus, not by following rules. Galatians 2:16 says, "A person is not justified by the works of the law, but by faith in Jesus Christ." You can't earn salvation—it's a gift received through faith.

## Freedom, Not Slavery

Paul says, "It is for freedom that Christ has set us free" (Galatians 5:1). Jesus set us free from the burden of trying to earn God's approval through rules. But freedom doesn't mean you can do whatever you want. Paul says, "Do not use your freedom to indulge the flesh; rather, serve one another humbly in love" (Galatians 5:13). Use your freedom to love and serve, not to sin.

## The Fruit of the Spirit

Galatians 5:22-23 lists the fruit of the Spirit: "love, joy, peace, forbearance, kindness, goodness, faithfulness, gentleness and self-control." When the Holy Spirit lives in you, these qualities grow. They're not things you produce by trying harder—they're the natural result of walking with the Spirit. Fun Fact: The "fruit" of the Spirit is singular (not "fruits")—all these qualities are one package that grows together!

## Ephesians: Our Identity in Christ

Ephesians is one of Paul's "prison epistles"—letters he wrote while under house arrest in Rome. It's a beautiful letter about who we are in Christ and how we should live.

## Blessed in Christ

Paul lists all the spiritual blessings we have in Christ. We're chosen, adopted, redeemed, forgiven, and sealed with the Holy Spirit. Ephesians 2:8-9 says, "For it is by grace you have been saved, through faith—and this is not from yourselves, it is the gift of God—not by works, so that no one can boast."

## We're God's Masterpiece

Ephesians 2:10 says, "For we are God's handiwork, created in Christ Jesus to do good works." The word "handiwork" can also be translated "masterpiece." You're God's masterpiece! He created you with a purpose.

## The Armor of God

One of the most famous passages is about the armor of God (Ephesians 6:10-18). We're in a spiritual battle, and we need God's armor: - Belt of truth - Live in truth, not lies - Breastplate of righteousness - Live rightly before God - Shoes of the gospel of peace - Be ready to share the gospel - Shield of faith - Trust God and resist doubt - Helmet of salvation - Remember you're saved - Sword of the Spirit - Use God's Word - Prayer - Pray constantly This armor protects us and equips us for spiritual battle. Put it on every day! Think About It: - Which piece of God's armor do you need most right now? The shield of faith? The sword of the Spirit? How can you "put it on" today?

## What We Learn from These Letters

Romans - Everyone needs Jesus. Salvation is by faith, not works. God's love is unstoppable. 1 Corinthians - Unity matters. Love is the greatest. Use your gifts. The resurrection is essential. 2 Corinthians - God comforts us in suffering. We're new creations. God's grace is sufficient. Galatians - We're saved by faith, not rules. Christ set us free. Walk by the Spirit. Ephesians - We're blessed in Christ. We're God's masterpiece. Put on the armor of God. All of these letters are incredibly practical—they're instruction for how to live as a follower of Jesus.

Activity Time: Draw yourself wearing the "Armor of God." Label each piece: belt of truth, breastplate of righteousness, shoes of peace, shield of faith, helmet of salvation, sword of the Spirit. Color it and put it on your wall to remind you to put on God's armor every day! For Parents: Read Galatians 5:22-23 (the fruit of the Spirit) together. For each fruit, discuss: "What does this look like in our family?" For example, "What does patience look like when your brother takes too long in the bathroom?" or "How do we show kindness to neighbors?" Make it practical and memorable.

# Chapter 15: Paul's Letters Part 2: Philippians through Thessalonians

What if you were writing a letter from prison? Would you complain about your situation? Feel sorry for yourself? Not Paul! When he writes to the church in Philippi from a Roman prison, his letter is full of joy. He uses the words "joy" and "rejoice" over 16 times in just four short chapters! Think about it. Paul is literally chained to a Roman guard 24 hours a day. He can't go where he wants. He doesn't know if he'll be executed or released. Yet he writes the most joyful letter in the New Testament! How? Because Paul's joy isn't based on his situation—it's based on his relationship with Jesus. In this chapter, we'll look at four more of Paul's letters: Philippians, Colossians, 1 Thessalonians, and 2 Thessalonians.

## Philippians: Joy in All Circumstances

The church in Philippi held a special place in Paul's heart. They were the first church he planted in Europe. They supported him financially, sent him gifts, and prayed for him faithfully. Paul writes from house arrest in Rome to thank them and encourage them.

## Paul's Prison Situation

Paul is under house arrest in Rome, chained to a Roman soldier 24 hours a day. These aren't just any soldiers—they're elite Praetorian guards from Caesar's palace, the emperor's personal troops. Every six hours, the guards rotate shifts, which means Paul has a captive audience! Literally! The guard can't leave. He has to stand there (or sit) chained to Paul while Paul prays, sings hymns, teaches visitors, and talks about Jesus constantly. Imagine being a Roman soldier expecting to guard a dangerous criminal, and instead you're chained to this joyful man who won't stop talking about how much Jesus loves you! Paul writes: "I want you to know, brothers and sisters, that what has happened to me has actually served to advance the gospel. As a result, it has become clear throughout the whole palace guard and to everyone else that I am in chains for Christ" (Philippians 1:12-13). The whole palace guard has heard about Jesus! Paul's imprisonment isn't stopping the gospel—it's spreading it to places it might never have reached!

Guards are hearing. Caesar's household is being impacted. Other Christians in Rome are being emboldened by Paul's courageous example. This teaches us an incredible lesson: God can use any situation—even the most difficult, unfair ones—to spread the gospel and accomplish His purposes. Your hardest circumstances might be God's greatest opportunities! Fun Fact: While imprisoned, Paul was chained to different Roman guards in 6-hour shifts—meaning dozens of soldiers heard the gospel firsthand!

## Rejoice Always!

Philippians 4:4 is one of the most famous verses: "Rejoice in the Lord always. I will say it again: Rejoice!" Paul doesn't just say it once—he repeats it for emphasis! What does it mean to "rejoice in the Lord"? Paul isn't saying, "Be happy about your problems." He's saying, "Find joy in your relationship with Jesus, no matter what's happening around you." In Philippians 4:11-13, Paul writes, "I have learned to be content whatever the circumstances... I can do all this through him who gives me strength." That last part—verse 13—is famous: "I can do all things through Christ who strengthens me." But understand what Paul means. He's not saying, "I can become a professional athlete just by believing harder." He's saying, "I can endure anything—plenty or poverty, freedom or chains—because Christ gives me strength." With Jesus, you can face anything life throws at you!

## The Mind of Christ

In Philippians 2:1-11, Paul gives one of the most beautiful descriptions of Jesus in the entire New Testament. Even though Jesus was God, He didn't cling to His rights and privileges. Instead, He "made himself nothing by taking the very nature of a servant... He humbled himself by becoming obedient to death—even death on a cross!" That's humility! And Paul says we should have the same attitude. We should think of others as more important than ourselves. We should be willing to serve, even when it's uncomfortable. Think About It: - Paul found joy even in prison. What's one hard situation you're facing? How can you find Jesus in the middle of it?

## Colossians: Jesus Is Supreme

The church in Colossae faced false teachers who said you needed Jesus plus something else. Paul writes to correct this error: Jesus is supreme, and He's all you need!

## Jesus Is Above All

Colossians 1:15-20 is one of the most powerful descriptions of Jesus in the entire Bible: "The Son is the image of the invisible God" - Jesus perfectly shows us what God is like. "For in him all things were created" - Jesus created everything! Angels, planets, animals, humans. "He is before all things, and in him all things hold together" - Jesus is holding every atom in your body together right now. Without Jesus, everything would fall apart! "For God was pleased to have all his fullness dwell in him" - All of God dwells in Jesus! After reading all of that, how could anyone think Jesus isn't enough? Fun Fact: When Paul says Jesus holds "all things" together, that includes atoms, molecules, planets, and galaxies—Jesus is the glue of the universe!

## Set Your Mind on Things Above

Colossians 3:1-2 says, "Set your hearts on things above, where Christ is... Set your minds on things above, not on earthly things." What does this mean? Focus on eternal things rather than temporary things. Value what God values. Instead of chasing popularity or stuff, chase after Jesus. Instead of living for today, live with eternity in mind. Then Paul gets specific. "Put to death" these behaviors: sexual immorality, anger, rage, malice, slander, lying. "Put on" these: compassion, kindness, humility, gentleness, patience, forgiveness, and love. It's like changing clothes. You take off the old, dirty clothes (sinful behaviors) and put on new, clean clothes (godly character).

## 1 Thessalonians: Living in Light of Jesus' Return

The church in Thessalonica was young when Paul wrote this letter. One main topic Paul addresses is the return of Jesus.

## The Return of Jesus

The Thessalonians were grieving and worried. Some believers in their church had died—maybe from persecution, illness, or old age—and they were wondering: "What happens to them? Will they miss out when Jesus returns? Will we ever see them again?" These questions were causing them deep grief. Paul writes to comfort them: "Brothers and sisters, we do not want you to be uninformed about those who sleep in death, or to grieve like the rest of mankind, who have no hope. For we believe that Jesus died and rose again, and so we believe that God will bring with Jesus those who have fallen asleep in him" (1 Thessalonians 4:13-14). Notice Paul calls death "sleep"—it's temporary, not permanent! And Christians don't grieve like people who have no hope. We grieve because we miss our loved ones, but we have hope because death isn't the end! Then Paul describes what will happen when Jesus returns: "For the Lord himself will come down from heaven, with a loud command, with the voice of the archangel and with the trumpet call of God, and the dead in Christ will rise first. After that, we who are still alive and are left will be caught up together with them in the clouds to meet the Lord in the air. And so we will be with the Lord forever" (1 Thessalonians 4:16-17). Imagine this scene! Jesus descends from heaven with a shout, with the archangel's voice, with God's trumpet blasting! First, believers who have died will be resurrected—their bodies raised and transformed. Then believers who are still alive will be "caught up"—suddenly lifted to meet Jesus in the air! This event is often called "the Rapture." All believers—dead and alive—will be reunited with Jesus forever! Death doesn't separate us from Jesus or from each other! Paul concludes: "Therefore encourage one another with these words." This is meant to give us hope and comfort! But when will Jesus return? Paul says it will come "like a thief in the night"—unexpectedly. So we should always be ready. Paul gives simple commands: "Rejoice always, pray continually, give thanks in all circumstances; for this is God's will for you in Christ Jesus" (1 Thessalonians 5:16-18). Think About It: - Jesus could return any day. If He came back today, what would you want to make sure you'd done?

## 2 Thessalonians: Clearing Up Confusion

Shortly after Paul's first letter, confusion arose. Someone had been teaching that the Day of the Lord (Jesus' return) had already happened! Paul writes to address this issue.

## The Day of the Lord Hasn't Happened Yet

Paul clarifies: "Don't let anyone deceive you in any way, for that day will not come until the rebellion occurs and the man of lawlessness is revealed" (2 Thessalonians 2:3). Certain things must happen before Jesus returns. There will be a great rebellion, and "the man of lawlessness" (often called the Antichrist) will appear. But ultimately, "The Lord Jesus will overthrow [him] with the breath of his mouth" (2 Thessalonians 2:8). Jesus wins!

## Work Hard While You Wait

Paul addresses people who had stopped working. He gives a blunt command: "The one who is unwilling to work shall not eat" (2 Thessalonians 3:10). The fact that Jesus is coming back doesn't mean we stop living responsibly. Work hard while you wait for Jesus' return. Fun Fact: Paul practiced what he preached—he supported himself by making tents while he traveled and preached the gospel!

## What We Learn from These Letters

Philippians - True joy comes from knowing Jesus, not from perfect circumstances. You can be content because Christ gives you strength. Have the humble, servant attitude of Jesus. Colossians - Jesus is supreme over everything. He's all you need! Set your mind on eternal things. Put off sinful behaviors and put on godly character. 1 Thessalonians - Jesus is coming back! Since we don't know when, live faithfully every day. Rejoice always, pray continually, and give thanks in all circumstances. 2 Thessalonians - The Day of the Lord hasn't happened yet. Work hard while you wait for Jesus' return!

Activity Time: Create a "Joy Jar." Find a jar or box and decorate it. Every day this week, write one thing you're thankful for on a slip of paper and put it in the jar. At the end of the week, read them all. This helps you practice "rejoice always, give thanks in all circumstances" like Paul taught! For

Parents: Discuss Philippians 4:13 together ("I can do all things through Christ"). Ask: "What does Paul mean by 'all things'?" Clarify it's about enduring any circumstance, not accomplishing anything we want. Share a time when God gave you strength to endure a hard situation. For Parents (Tip 2): Talk about Jesus' return using 1 Thessalonians 4:13-18. Ask: "If Jesus came back today, what would you be excited about?" Help your child see Jesus' return as hopeful, not scary. Discuss: "How should we live while we wait?"

# Chapter 16: Paul's Letters Part 3: Timothy, Titus, and Philemon

"Don't let anyone look down on you because you are young, but set an example for the believers in speech, in conduct, in love, in faith and in purity." That's 1 Timothy 4:12, and it's one of the most empowering verses in the Bible for young people! Have you ever felt like you're too young to make a difference? Timothy probably felt the same way! He was a young leader in a church full of older people. But Paul's message to Timothy—and to you—is clear: age is just a number. What matters is your heart for God. In this chapter, we'll look at Paul's final four letters: 1 Timothy, 2 Timothy, Titus, and Philemon.

## 1 Timothy: Instructions for a Young Leader

Timothy was Paul's protégé—his spiritual son and closest ministry partner. Their relationship started years earlier on Paul's second missionary journey when Paul visited Lystra, Timothy's hometown. Timothy was probably a teenager or young man at the time. His father was Greek (a non-believer), but his mother Eunice and grandmother Lois were devout Jewish believers who had carefully taught Timothy the Hebrew Scriptures from the time he was a small child. When Paul met this young man whose faith was genuine and whose reputation was excellent, Paul saw tremendous potential. He invited Timothy to join his missionary team, and Timothy became like a beloved son to him—traveling with Paul, learning from him, carrying his letters, and representing him to churches. Now, years later, Paul has left Timothy with a huge responsibility: leading the church in Ephesus, one of the largest and most important cities in the Roman Empire. Ephesus wasn't an easy assignment! The city was full of idol worship (including the massive temple of Artemis, one of the seven wonders of the ancient world), occult practices, sexual immorality, and false teachers infiltrating the church with dangerous doctrines. And Timothy was young—probably in his early to mid-thirties, which was considered quite young for such a significant leadership role in that culture. Timothy also seems to have struggled with timidity and health issues. So Paul writes this letter to encourage Timothy, give him practical guidance, and remind him of his calling.

## Don't Be Intimidated by Your Age

Paul tells Timothy not to let anyone look down on him because he's young. Instead, he should set an example in five areas: speech (the words you use), conduct (the way you act), love (how you treat others), faith (your trust in God), and purity (living a clean life). Notice Paul doesn't say, "Prove you're mature by acting older." He says, "Set an example." When people see you loving others, trusting God, speaking truth, and living purely, they won't care how old you are! Fun Fact: Timothy was probably around 30-35 years old—young for a church leader in his culture, but old enough to vote today!

## Fight the Good Fight

Paul tells Timothy to "fight the good fight of the faith" (1 Timothy 6:12). Following Jesus isn't always easy. You might face peer pressure. You might be tempted to give up. That's when you need to remember: you're in a fight worth fighting! You're not fighting against people. You're fighting to keep trusting Jesus and living for Him even when it's difficult.

## The Love of Money

One of Paul's famous warnings concerns money: "The love of money is a root of all kinds of evil" (1 Timothy 6:10). Notice Paul doesn't say money itself is evil. Money is neutral. But loving money, making it your highest priority—that's when it becomes dangerous. Instead, Paul tells Timothy to "pursue righteousness, godliness, faith, love, endurance and gentleness" (1 Timothy 6:11). Chase after the things that really matter! Think About It: - Paul told Timothy to set an example in five areas: speech, conduct, love, faith, and purity. Which of these five is hardest for you?

## 2 Timothy: Paul's Final Words

2 Timothy is probably the last letter Paul ever wrote, and you can feel the weight of finality in every line. Paul is in prison in Rome again—but this time is vastly different from his earlier house arrest. Now he's locked in the Mamertine Prison, a dark, cold, underground dungeon beneath Rome. It's winter, and he's cold, asking Timothy to bring his cloak. The Roman emperor Nero has launched a vicious persecution against Christians, using them as scapegoats after the great fire of Rome. Christians are being thrown

to lions, burned as human torches in Nero's gardens, and crucified along Roman roads. Paul knows his trial will almost certainly end in execution. This letter reads like a man's final words to his beloved son—full of raw emotion, hard-won wisdom, and urgent pleading. Paul writes about feeling abandoned and lonely. He says, "Demas, because he loved this world, has deserted me... Only Luke is with me" (2 Timothy 4:10-11). Most of his friends and coworkers have left—some for legitimate ministry reasons, but some (like Demas) because they loved the world more than Christ. Paul longs to see Timothy one more time before he dies. Yet despite the cold, the loneliness, the chains, and the approaching execution, Paul's faith burns as bright as ever. He's not bitter. He's not despairing. He's finishing strong!

## Pass It On

Paul tells Timothy, "The things you have heard me say... entrust to reliable people who will also be qualified to teach others" (2 Timothy 2:2). Look at the chain: Paul taught Timothy, Timothy should teach reliable people, and they should teach others. That's four generations in one verse! This is how the gospel spreads—each generation teaching the next. Someone taught you about Jesus. Now it's your turn to pass it on!

## Don't Be Ashamed

Paul encourages Timothy not to be ashamed of the gospel. This must have been a temptation—after all, Paul was imprisoned! But Paul reminds him: "God has not given us a spirit of fear, but of power, of love, and of a sound mind" (2 Timothy 1:7, NKJV). Fear says, "What will people think?" But God gives us power—the ability to do what's right even when it's scary. God gives us love—stronger than fear of rejection. God gives us a sound mind—clarity to think clearly and act wisely. Don't be afraid to stand up for Jesus! Fun Fact: 2 Timothy was written from the Mamertine Prison in Rome—a dark, underground dungeon where Paul awaited execution!

## I Have Fought the Good Fight

Paul's closing words are powerful: "I have fought the good fight, I have finished the race, I have kept the faith. Now there is in store for me the crown of righteousness" (2 Timothy 4:7-8). Picture Paul, an old man in chains, facing execution. He could be bitter. Instead, he's looking back with satisfaction and forward with hope. He fought the good fight—he didn't give up. He finished the race—he persevered to the end. He kept the faith—he never stopped trusting Jesus. And now, a crown awaits him! And Paul says this crown isn't just for him—it's for everyone who loves Jesus and eagerly waits for His return. That includes you! Think About It: - Paul said "I have fought the good fight, finished the race, kept the faith." What would it look like for you to finish strong?

## Titus: Setting Things in Order

Titus was another of Paul's co-workers. Paul left him on the island of Crete to organize the churches there. Crete had a reputation for being difficult. One of their own prophets said, "Cretans are always liars, evil brutes, lazy gluttons" (Titus 1:12). Not exactly flattering! The churches needed solid leadership and clear teaching. That's where Titus comes in.

## Grace Changes Us

Titus 2:11-12 is a key passage: "For the grace of God has appeared that offers salvation to all people. It teaches us to say 'No' to ungodliness and worldly passions, and to live self-controlled, upright and godly lives." Notice what grace does. It doesn't just forgive us—it teaches us! God's grace shows us how to live. It helps us say no to sin and yes to righteousness. When you truly understand how much God loves you and what Jesus did for you, it changes how you want to live. Fun Fact: The island of Crete is about 160 miles long—Titus had to travel all over to organize multiple churches!

## Philemon: A Lesson in Forgiveness

Philemon is the shortest of Paul's letters—just 25 verses. But it contains a powerful message about forgiveness.

## The Story

Philemon is a wealthy Christian who owns a slave named Onesimus. Onesimus apparently stole from Philemon and ran away—a serious crime. Runaway slaves could be severely punished, even executed. But Onesimus ended up in Rome and met Paul. Paul told him about Jesus, and Onesimus became a Christian! Now Paul faces a dilemma. He would love to keep Onesimus to help in his ministry. But he knows the right thing is to send Onesimus back to Philemon. So Paul writes this letter asking for forgiveness.

## A Masterclass in Grace

Paul's approach is brilliant. He doesn't command Philemon to forgive. Instead, he appeals on the basis of love and friendship. Paul says, "I am sending him—who is my very heart—back to you... no longer as a slave, but better than a slave, as a dear brother" (Philemon 12, 16). Onesimus is now part of God's family! Then Paul makes an incredible offer: "If he has done you any wrong or owes you anything, charge it to me" (Philemon 18). Paul is offering to take Onesimus' debt on himself. Does this sound familiar? It's a picture of what Jesus did for us! We owed a debt we couldn't pay. Jesus said, "Charge it to me." And He did, on the cross. Church tradition says Philemon not only forgave Onesimus but eventually set him free. Some historians believe Onesimus later became the bishop of Ephesus! Think About It: - Paul asked Philemon to forgive Onesimus completely. Is there someone you need to forgive?

## What We Learn from These Letters

1 Timothy - Don't let your age stop you from serving God. Set an example in speech, conduct, love, faith, and purity. Fight the good fight—don't give up! Watch out for the love of money. 2 Timothy - Pass on what you've learned. Don't be ashamed of the gospel. God hasn't given you fear but power, love, and a sound mind. Finish strong! Titus - Grace doesn't just forgive—it teaches us how to live! Be intentional about doing good works. Philemon - Forgiveness is costly but beautiful. When we forgive, we reflect the amazing forgiveness Jesus showed us.

Activity Time: Create a "Finish Strong" poster. Draw a race finish line. Above it, write 2 Timothy 4:7-8 ("I have fought the good fight..."). Below it, list three ways YOU want to finish strong in your faith. Put it on your wall as a reminder! For Parents: Read 1 Timothy 4:12 together. Discuss the five areas Timothy should set an example: speech, conduct, love, faith, purity. For each area, brainstorm one practical way your child can set an example this week (e.g., "speech" = speak kindly to siblings).

# Chapter 17: Hebrews: Jesus Is Better

What if there's a book in the Bible that's like a bridge connecting the Old Testament and the New Testament? That's Hebrews! This book shows how everything in the Old Testament points to Jesus and how Jesus is better than everything that came before. Hebrews was written to Jewish Christians who were facing intense persecution for believing in Jesus. They were losing their jobs, their property was being confiscated, some faced imprisonment, and they endured constant pressure from family and community to abandon Christ and return to Judaism. The temptation was real: "If I just go back to the synagogue, life will be easier. I can keep my job, my reputation, my relationships." They were wondering: Is following Jesus really worth all this suffering? Can't I just go back to following Moses and the Law? The author's answer thunders through every chapter with a resounding YES! Jesus is infinitely greater than anything they left behind. Why would you trade the Reality for mere shadows? Why exchange the Son of God for religious rituals? The entire book builds an overwhelming case: Jesus is superior to every single thing in the Old Testament system!

## Jesus Is Better Than Everything

The main theme of Hebrews is simple: Jesus is better. Better than the angels. Better than Moses. Better than the old priesthood. Better than the old sacrifices.

## Better Than Angels

Hebrews starts by saying Jesus is superior to angels. Why? Because angels were highly revered in Jewish thought. But Hebrews 1:3 says Jesus "is the radiance of God's glory and the exact representation of his being, sustaining all things by his powerful word." Think about that! Jesus radiates God's glory like the sun radiates light. He perfectly represents who God is. And He holds the entire universe together! Angels are created beings who serve God, but Jesus is God's eternal Son. Fun Fact: Angels worship Jesus—they don't expect us to worship them! (See Revelation 22:8-9)

## Better Than Moses

Moses was a national hero to the Jewish people. He led them out of Egypt, parted the Red Sea, and gave them God's law. But Hebrews says Jesus is greater! Hebrews explains: Moses was a faithful servant in God's house, but Jesus is the Son over God's house (Hebrews 3:5-6). Moses was like a trusted employee. Jesus is the Master's Son who owns the house! Moses pointed people to God and delivered God's words. But Jesus is God! Moses gave the old covenant, but Jesus established the new covenant.

## A Better High Priest

In the Old Testament, the high priest would enter the Most Holy Place once a year to make atonement for the people's sins. This ritual had to be repeated year after year because animal sacrifices couldn't permanently take away sin. But Jesus is a better high priest! First, Jesus is perfect and sinless. Old Testament priests had to offer sacrifices for their own sins first. Jesus never sinned, so He didn't need to sacrifice for Himself. Second—and this is the best part—Jesus doesn't have to keep offering sacrifices over and over. He offered Himself once for all! Hebrews 9:12 says, "He did not enter by means of the blood of goats and calves; but he entered the Most Holy Place once for all by his own blood, thus obtaining eternal redemption." The old priests kept offering the same sacrifices day after day, year after year. Jesus offered one sacrifice—Himself—one time, and it completely paid for all sins for all time. It's done! And now Jesus is in heaven, interceding for us before the Father. When we sin, Jesus speaks up for us. We have the best High Priest imaginable! Think About It: - Jesus' one sacrifice paid for all your sins—past, present, and future. How does that change how you feel about mistakes you've made?

## A Better Covenant

The old covenant, given at Mount Sinai, was based on laws written on stone tablets. It told people what to do, but it didn't give them the power to do it. People kept breaking the law because their hearts weren't changed. The new covenant is different. It's based on God's law written on our hearts by the Holy Spirit. God changes us from the inside out! And here's the most amazing part—Hebrews 8:12 says, "For I will forgive their wickedness and will remember their sins no more." Under the new covenant, God completely forgives our sins. He removes them—as far as the east is from the west! And He remembers them no more. Fun Fact: The phrase "new covenant" appears over 20 times in the New Testament—it's central to understanding what Jesus accomplished!

## The Hall of Faith

Hebrews 11 is one of the most inspiring chapters in the entire Bible—sometimes called the "Hall of Faith." Imagine walking through a grand hallway lined with portraits of spiritual heroes, each one with a plaque describing their incredible faith. That's what this chapter feels like! The author lists people from the Old Testament who lived by extraordinary faith: Abel, Enoch, Noah, Abraham, Sarah, Isaac, Jacob, Joseph, Moses, Rahab, Gideon, Barak, Samson, Jephthah, David, Samuel, and the prophets! The chapter opens with one of the most famous definitions of faith ever written: "Now faith is confidence in what we hope for and assurance about what we do not see" (Hebrews 11:1). Faith isn't wishful thinking or blind optimism. It's being absolutely certain about what God has promised even when you don't have physical proof yet. It's trusting God's character and His Word so completely that you act on it! Then comes the parade of heroes: "By faith Abel offered God a better sacrifice than Cain did"—and even though he died, "by faith he still speaks" (v.4). "By faith Enoch was taken from this life, so that he did not experience death"—he walked so closely with God that God just took him to heaven! (v.5). "By faith Noah, when warned about things not yet seen, in holy fear built an ark to save his family"—imagine spending decades building a massive boat when it had never even rained, while everyone mocked you! (v.7). "By faith Abraham, when called to go to a place he would later receive as his inheritance, obeyed and went, even though he did not know where he was going" (v.8). He left his comfortable home and became a nomad living in tents, looking forward to "the city with foundations, whose architect and builder is God" (v.10). "By faith Abraham, even though he was past age—and Sarah herself was barren—was enabled to become a father because he considered him faithful who had made the promise" (v.11). When Abraham was 100 and Sarah was 90, they had Isaac! "By faith Moses, when he had grown up, refused to be known as the son of Pharaoh's daughter. He chose to be mistreated along with the people of God rather than to enjoy the fleeting pleasures of sin" (v.24-25). Moses gave up being a prince of Egypt—wealth, power, luxury—to suffer with slaves! "By faith the prostitute Rahab, because she welcomed the spies, was not killed with those who were disobedient" (v.31)—she risked everything to protect God's people. Then the author speeds up, almost breathless: "And what more shall I say? I do not have time to tell about Gideon, Barak, Samson, Jephthah, David, Samuel and the prophets, who through faith conquered kingdoms, administered justice, and gained what was promised; who shut the mouths of lions, quenched the fury of the flames, and escaped the edge of the sword; whose weakness was turned to strength; and who became powerful in battle and routed foreign armies" (v.32-34). But then comes the sobering reality—not everyone's faith led to earthly deliverance. Some "were tortured, refusing to be released so that they might gain an even better resurrection. Some faced jeers and flogging, and even chains and imprisonment. They were put to death by stoning; they were sawed in two; they were killed by the sword. They went about in sheepskins and goatskins, destitute, persecuted and mistreated" (v.35-37). Yet through it all, they trusted God! The conclusion is powerful: "These were all commended for their faith, yet none of them received what had been promised, since God had planned something better for us so that only together with us would they be made perfect" (v.39-40). These Old Testament heroes were looking forward to something—or Someone—they never fully saw in their lifetimes. They were looking forward to Jesus! And now we have Him! The story isn't complete without us—we're all part of God's grand plan of faith! Think About It: - The heroes of faith trusted God even when they couldn't see the outcome. What's one area where you need to trust God more?

## Run the Race

Hebrews 12:1 says, "Therefore, since we are surrounded by such a great cloud of witnesses, let us throw off everything that hinders and the sin that so easily entangles. And let us run with perseverance the race marked out for us." Picture a huge stadium packed with people cheering you on. That's what these heroes of faith are like! They ran their race faithfully, and now it's our turn. So let's throw off everything that slows us down—sin, doubt, fear, distractions—and run our race with perseverance, keeping our eyes on Jesus! And the Christian life isn't a sprint—it's a marathon! It requires endurance. You can't just run fast for a little while—you have to keep going mile after mile. The key is to keep your eyes on Jesus, "the pioneer and perfecter of faith" (Hebrews 12:2). Jesus is both the trailblazer who ran the race ahead of us and the one who completes our faith. He's both the example we follow and the one who gives us strength to finish. Think About It: - Hebrews talks about "the sin that so easily entangles." What's one thing that keeps tripping you up? How can you "throw it off"?

## What We Learn from Hebrews

Jesus is better than everything. Angels, Moses, priests, sacrifices—Jesus surpasses them all! He's the fulfillment of everything the Old Testament pointed to. Jesus' sacrifice is complete. We don't need to keep offering sacrifices. Jesus died once for all. Our sins are forgiven! Faith is essential. The heroes of Hebrews 11 trusted God, and we're called to do the same. Keep believing, even when you can't see what God is doing! Keep running the race. The Christian life requires perseverance. There will be times you want to quit. Don't give up! Keep your eyes on Jesus!

Activity Time: Create a "Hall of Faith" poster. Draw a hallway with frames on the walls. In each frame, write the name of a faith hero from Hebrews 11 (Abel, Noah, Abraham, Moses, etc.) and one word describing their faith (obedient, brave, trusting). Add an empty frame at the end with YOUR name—you're part of the story! For Parents: Read Hebrews 12:1-2 together about running the race. Discuss: "What are some things that slow us down spiritually?" (e.g., too much screen time, laziness, busyness). Ask: "What's one thing we can 'throw off' as a family to run better?" Make a practical plan together.

# Chapter 18: Living It Out: James and Peter's Letters

Talk is cheap. You can say you believe in Jesus, but if your life doesn't show it, what good is that? That's the message of James. He's very direct: "Faith by itself, if it is not accompanied by action, is dead" (James 2:17). Real faith produces real change in how you live. Have you ever met someone who talks a big game but never follows through? James is saying faith can be like that too. You can claim to believe in Jesus, but if your life doesn't reflect that belief—if you're not living differently because of Jesus—then something's wrong. In this chapter, we'll look at the letters of James and Peter (1 and 2 Peter). These letters are intensely practical—all about living out your faith in everyday situations.

## James: Faith That Works

James was Jesus' half-brother—they grew up in the same household in Nazareth! Can you imagine growing up with Jesus as your older brother? Watching Him be perfectly obedient to your parents, never sin, always do what's right? Yet during Jesus' three years of public ministry, James didn't believe Jesus was the Messiah. In fact, John 7:5 specifically says, "even his own brothers did not believe in him." Imagine the tension—Jesus claiming to be God's Son while His own family thought He was mistaken or deluded. But everything changed after the resurrection. Jesus personally appeared to James (1 Corinthians 15:7), and James became a completely devoted believer! And when James believed, he went all in—no halfway commitment! He rose to become one of the key leaders of the Jerusalem church, working alongside Peter and John. Church tradition says people nicknamed him "James the Just" because of his reputation for incredible righteousness and constant prayer. His letter isn't theological or abstract—it's intensely practical, like a collection of hard-hitting wisdom for daily living. James wants to know: Is your faith real? Does it actually change how you live?

## Faith and Works Go Together

James says, "Show me your faith without deeds, and I will show you my faith by my deeds" (James 2:18). He's throwing down a challenge: You say you have faith? Prove it! Show me! Let's be clear: James is NOT saying you're saved by good works. Paul made it crystal clear that salvation is by grace through faith, not by works. But James is saying that real faith naturally produces good works. Think of it like this: If you plant an apple seed and it's truly alive, it will eventually produce apples. If it never produces fruit, something's wrong. Faith is similar. Real, living faith in Jesus will eventually produce the fruit of good works—not because we're trying to earn salvation, but because we're changed by grace! Fun Fact: James uses over 50 commands in just 5 chapters—more than any other New Testament book! He's all about action!

## Control Your Tongue

James dedicates significant space in chapter 3 to talking about the tongue—our words. And he doesn't sugarcoat how dangerous uncontrolled speech can be! He starts by warning that teachers will be judged more strictly because they use words to influence others (James 3:1). Then he gives powerful illustrations about how something so small can have such massive impact. "When we put bits into the mouths of horses to make them obey us, we can turn the whole animal. Or take ships as an example. Although they are so large and are driven by strong winds, they are steered by a very small rudder wherever the pilot wants to go" (James 3:3-4). A tiny bit controls a thousand-pound horse. A small rudder steers a massive ship. The point? Small things have huge influence! "Likewise, the tongue is a small part of the body, but it makes great boasts. Consider what a great forest is set on fire by a small spark. The tongue also is a fire, a world of evil among the parts of the body. It corrupts the whole body, sets the whole course of one's life on fire, and is itself set on fire by hell" (James 3:5-6). Those are strong, vivid words! One small spark—one careless word, one cruel comment—can start a raging fire of destruction. Your tongue can ruin friendships, destroy reputations, break hearts, and cause damage that lasts for years. Then James points out the irony: "All kinds of animals, birds, reptiles and sea creatures are being tamed and have been tamed by mankind, but no human being can tame the tongue. It is a restless evil, full of deadly poison" (James 3:7-8). We've trained lions, dolphins, and elephants—but we can't fully control our own tongues! They're "restless"—always ready to blurt out something destructive. They're "full of deadly poison"—words that kill joy, destroy confidence, and spread hurt. Here's the most convicting part: "With the tongue we praise our Lord and Father, and with it we curse human beings, who have been made in God's likeness. Out of the same mouth come praise and cursing. My brothers and sisters, this should not be! Can both fresh water and salt water flow from the same spring?" (James 3:9-11). James is calling out hypocrisy. We use our mouths to sing worship songs to God on Sunday morning—"How great is our God!"—and then on Monday afternoon we use the same mouth to gossip about someone, say mean things to our sibling, or complain bitterly. James says bluntly: "This should not be!" It's inconsistent! It's like expecting fresh water and salt water to come from the same spring—it's impossible! The challenge is clear but difficult: tame your tongue! James admits it's nearly impossible for humans to control completely, which means we desperately need God's help. Pray like David did: "Set a guard over my mouth, Lord; keep watch over the door of my lips" (Psalm 141:3). Before you speak, pause and ask yourself three questions: Is it true? Is it kind? Is it necessary? If the answer to any of these is "no," don't say it! Use your words to build people up, not tear them down. Think About It: - James says we praise God and curse people with the same tongue. When's the last time your words hurt someone? How can you use words to build people up today?

## Be Quick to Listen, Slow to Speak, Slow to Anger

James 1:19 gives advice that could transform your relationships: "Everyone should be quick to listen, slow to speak and slow to anger." Quick to listen means really hearing what someone is saying. Slow to speak means think before you speak. Don't react immediately. Slow to anger means don't let anger control you. When you're angry, you rarely do what's right. Imagine how different your home, school, and friendships would be if you followed this advice! Fun Fact: James was written around 45-50 AD, making it possibly the oldest book in the New Testament!

# 1 Peter: Hope in Suffering

Peter, Jesus' disciple who once denied Him three times, writes to encourage believers suffering persecution. This is the same Peter who was brash and impulsive, who sank when he tried to walk on water. But Jesus restored Peter, and Peter became a pillar of the early church.

## Living Hope

Peter starts by praising God for giving us "new birth into a living hope through the resurrection of Jesus Christ from the dead" (1 Peter 1:3). Because Jesus rose from the dead, defeating death forever, we have hope that can never die! What are we hoping for? Our inheritance "kept in heaven for you" (1 Peter 1:4). Unlike earthly inheritances that can be stolen or destroyed, our heavenly inheritance is imperishable (won't rot), undefiled (won't be corrupted), and unfading (won't lose its beauty). And it's kept safe in heaven!

## Trials Refine Your Faith

Peter says trials test your faith like fire refines gold (1 Peter 1:7). When gold is heated, impurities rise to the surface and are removed, leaving pure gold. Similarly, when you go through hard times, it strengthens genuine faith. Peter says, "In all this you greatly rejoice, though now for a little while you may have had to suffer grief in all kinds of trials" (1 Peter 1:6). Trials are temporary ("a little while"), and God uses them for good.

## You Are Chosen

1 Peter 2:9 is powerful: "But you are a chosen people, a royal priesthood, a holy nation, God's special possession." You're chosen by God—hand-picked! You're royal—part of God's royal family! You're a priest—you have direct access to God! You're God's special possession—treasured by Him! Your identity isn't based on what others think. It's based on who God says you are! Think About It: - Peter says you're "chosen" and "God's special possession." How does knowing God chose YOU change how you see yourself?

## Cast Your Anxiety on God

One of the most comforting verses is 1 Peter 5:7: "Cast all your anxiety on him because he cares for you." "Cast" means to throw, to get rid of. Take all your worries and throw them on God! Why? Because He cares for you! When you're worried about school, friendships, family, or the future, give it to God in prayer. He's big enough to handle your problems!

## 2 Peter: Be on Guard

In his second letter, Peter warns about false teachers and encourages believers to grow. Peter knows he'll die soon, and he wants to make sure believers are prepared.

## Grow in Grace and Knowledge

2 Peter 1:8 lists qualities to add to your faith: goodness, knowledge, self-control, perseverance, godliness, mutual affection, and love. "For if you possess these qualities in increasing measure, they will keep you from being ineffective." Think of it like climbing a ladder. Start with faith, then add goodness, then knowledge, and so on. Keep growing! Don't stay stagnant!

## The Day of the Lord

Peter talks about Jesus' return. Some people mock and say, "Where is this 'coming' he promised?" But Peter explains that God's timing is different. "With the Lord a day is like a thousand years, and a thousand years are like a day" (2 Peter 3:8). And God isn't slow—He's patient! He's giving people more time to turn to Him. "The Lord is... patient with you, not wanting anyone to perish, but everyone to come to repentance" (2 Peter 3:9). The day of the Lord will come "like a thief"—unexpected, sudden. Then God will create "a new heaven and a new earth, where righteousness dwells" (2 Peter 3:13). That's our hope! Think About It: - Peter says to "grow in grace and knowledge." What's one way you can grow spiritually this week?

## What We Learn from James and Peter

James - Faith without works is dead. Real faith produces action. Control your tongue—your words have power. Be quick to listen, slow to speak, slow to anger. 1 Peter - You have living hope because of Jesus' resurrection! Trials refine your faith like fire refines gold. You're chosen by God! Cast all your anxiety on God—He cares for you! 2 Peter - Keep growing in faith! Beware of false teachers. Jesus is coming back—live holy lives while you wait!

Activity Time: Make a "Words Have Power" reminder. Cut out a large speech bubble from paper. On one side, write negative words (gossip, lies, mean words). On the other side, write positive words (encouragement, truth, kindness). Flip it to the positive side and put it on your mirror to remind you to use words wisely! For Parents: Read 1 Peter 5:7 together about casting anxiety on God. Ask your child: "What's something you're worried about?" Pray together and literally act out "casting" the worry to God by writing it on paper, crumpling it, and throwing it in the trash. Discuss how God handles what we give Him.

# Chapter 19: Love and Truth: John's Letters and Jude

"God is love." Those three simple words, found in 1 John 4:8, capture the heart of John's message. John, the disciple who called himself "the one Jesus loved," writes to remind believers that love is at the center of everything. Think about John's journey. He was one of Jesus' closest friends. He leaned on Jesus' chest at the Last Supper. He stood at the foot of the cross when Jesus died. He ran to the empty tomb on resurrection morning. After decades of following Jesus, John's message is simple: God is love, and if we know God, we'll love others. In this chapter, we'll look at John's three short letters and the even shorter letter from Jude.

## 1 John: Love One Another

John's first letter dives right in, talking about "the Word of life" (Jesus) whom they've seen, heard, and touched. John was an eyewitness to Jesus' life!

## God Is Light

John says, "God is light; in him there is no darkness at all" (1 John 1:5). Light represents truth, purity, and holiness. Darkness represents sin, lies, and evil. John's point: God is completely pure. So if we claim to have fellowship with God but walk in darkness (living in sin), we're fooling ourselves! But if we walk in the light—living in truth, pursuing holiness—we have fellowship with God. And "the blood of Jesus, his Son, purifies us from all sin" (1 John 1:7). Does this mean we have to be perfect? No! John says, "If we claim to be without sin, we deceive ourselves" (1 John 1:8). Everyone sins! But here's the good news: "If we confess our sins, he is faithful and just and will forgive us our sins and purify us from all unrighteousness" (1 John 1:9). When you sin, confess it to God, and He will forgive you! Fun Fact: 1 John is sometimes called "the love letter" because the word "love" appears over 40 times in just 5 chapters!

## Love God, Love Others

John makes a bold statement: you can't love God while hating other people. "Whoever claims to love God yet hates a brother or sister is a liar. For whoever does not love their brother and sister, whom they have seen, cannot love God, whom they have not seen" (1 John 4:20). Think about the logic: If you can't love a person you can see, how can you claim to love God whom you can't see? And love isn't just warm feelings—it's action. "This is how we know what love is: Jesus Christ laid down his life for us. And we ought to lay down our lives for our brothers and sisters" (1 John 3:16). John gives a practical example: "If anyone has material possessions and sees a brother or sister in need but has no pity on them, how can the love of God be in that person? Dear children, let us not love with words or speech but with actions and in truth" (1 John 3:17-18). Real love acts! Think About It: - John says love is shown through actions, not just words. What's one way you can show love through action this week?

## You Can Know You're Saved

One of John's primary purposes in writing this letter is to give believers absolute certainty about their salvation. Near the end of the letter, he states his purpose explicitly: "I write these things to you who believe in the name of the Son of God so that you may know that you have eternal life" (1 John 5:13). Notice that crucial word: "know"—not hope, not think, not wonder, but KNOW with certainty! John wants you to have rock-solid assurance! You don't have to spend your Christian life wondering anxiously, "Am I really saved? Did I pray the right words? Was my faith strong enough? What if I'm not really a Christian?" John says you can know—really, truly know—that you have eternal life! But how can you know for sure? Throughout his letter, John provides three clear tests—evidences that reveal whether your faith is genuine: The Belief Test: "Who is it that overcomes the world? Only the one who believes that Jesus is the Son of God" (1 John 5:5). Do you genuinely believe that Jesus is the Son of God who came in human flesh, lived a sinless life, died on the cross for your sins, and rose from the dead? Do you confess Him as your Savior and Lord? Real saving faith involves confessing Jesus. The Obedience Test: "We know that we have come to know him if we keep his commands. Whoever says, 'I know him,' but does not do what he commands is a liar"

(1 John 2:3-4). Do you strive to obey God's commands? Notice John doesn't say you have to be perfect—none of us are! But is there a genuine pattern of wanting to please God? Do you care about living righteously? When you sin, are you grieved and do you repent? Real Christians have a desire for obedience, even when they fail. The Love Test: "We know that we have passed from death to life, because we love each other. Anyone who does not love remains in death" (1 John 3:14). Do you love other believers? Not perfectly—we all struggle with selfishness—but is there evidence of love growing in your life? Do you care about other Christians? Real faith produces love for God's family. If you've genuinely put your faith in Jesus, and you see these evidences in your life—even imperfectly—you can have absolute confidence that you're saved! Your salvation doesn't depend on perfect feelings or flawless performance. It depends on Jesus and His finished work on the cross. Trust Him, and rest in the assurance that you have eternal life! If you believe in Jesus, strive to obey Him, and love others, you can be confident you're saved!

## God Is Love

1 John 4:8 gives us one of the most profound statements in Scripture: "Whoever does not love does not know God, because God is love." God isn't just loving—He IS love. Love isn't just something God does—it's who He is at His very core. And because we're His children, we should love like He does. Here's how God showed His love: "This is love: not that we loved God, but that he loved us and sent his Son as an atoning sacrifice for our sins" (1 John 4:10). We didn't love God first—He loved us first! That's incredible love! Fun Fact: The apostle John lived longer than all the other apostles—probably into his 90s, the last surviving eyewitness of Jesus! By the time he wrote these letters, he was an elderly man, a revered "elder" of the church. All the other apostles had been martyred decades earlier—Peter crucified, Paul beheaded, James killed by Herod. John alone remained, carrying the precious memories of walking with Jesus. He spent his final years in Ephesus (in modern-day Turkey), teaching, writing, and constantly emphasizing one central theme: love. Church tradition says John became so frail that he had to be carried into church meetings. When asked to speak, he would simply repeat over and over, "Little children, love one another." When people asked why he always said the same thing, John replied, "Because it is the Lord's command, and if this alone is done, it is enough."

That's the heart of an old man who had spent a lifetime learning what matters most!

## 2 John: Walk in Love and Truth

John's second letter is super short—just 13 verses! Despite its brevity, it packs a powerful message: walk in both love and truth.

## Truth and Love Together

John rejoices that some are "walking in the truth." But he also commands them to love one another: "And now, dear lady, I am not writing you a new command but one we have had from the beginning. I ask that we love one another" (2 John 5). Here's the key: Truth and love go together! Truth without love is harsh and judgmental. Love without truth is weak and compromising. We need both! Speak the truth in love. Love people with genuine truth. John also warns about false teachers who deny that Jesus came in the flesh. He says, "If anyone comes to you and does not bring this teaching, do not take them into your house" (2 John 10). Don't support false teachers!

## 3 John: Supporting Faithful Workers

John's third letter is written to a man named Gaius. John praises Gaius for "walking in the truth" and showing hospitality to traveling teachers spreading the gospel. John says, "We ought therefore to show hospitality to such people so that we may work together for the truth" (3 John 8). When you support faithful gospel workers, you become a partner in their ministry! But John also mentions Diotrephes, who "loves to be first." Diotrephes spreads gossip and kicks people out of church. He's a terrible example of selfish leadership. Instead, John commends Demetrius, who has a good reputation and lives according to the truth. The message: Support those who faithfully serve Jesus. Don't follow people who are selfish and divisive. Think About It: - John says truth and love go together. Are you better at speaking truth or showing love? How can you grow in the other area?

## Jude: Contend for the Faith

Jude is the last letter before Revelation. Jude was another of Jesus' half-brothers. He originally planned to write about salvation, but he felt urgently compelled to warn believers about false teachers.

## Stand Firm

Jude urges believers to "contend for the faith that was once for all entrusted to God's holy people" (Jude 3). "Contend" means to fight for, defend vigorously. The faith has been "once for all" delivered—it's complete, not changing. Don't let false teachers twist it! Jude is sounding an alarm: The gospel is under attack! Fight for the truth!

## False Teachers Condemned

Jude doesn't hold back in describing false teachers. He uses vivid imagery: "Shepherds who feed only themselves"—they care only about themselves. "Clouds without rain"—they promise something good but deliver nothing. "Autumn trees, without fruit"—completely useless and lifeless. These false teachers are dangerous! They twist grace into permission to sin.

## Build Yourself Up

But Jude also encourages. He tells believers: "But you, dear friends, by building yourselves up in your most holy faith and praying in the Holy Spirit, keep yourselves in God's love as you wait for the mercy of our Lord Jesus Christ" (Jude 20-21). Build yourself up in the faith—keep learning and growing. Pray in the Holy Spirit—let God's Spirit guide your prayers. Keep yourself in God's love—stay close to Him. Wait for Jesus to return—your ultimate hope! Fun Fact: Jude has one of the most beautiful benedictions in the Bible (verses 24-25): "To him who is able to keep you from stumbling..."!

## The Doxology

Jude ends with one of the most beautiful blessings: "To him who is able to keep you from stumbling and to present you before his glorious presence without fault and with great joy—to the only God our Savior be glory, majesty, power and authority, through Jesus Christ our Lord, before all ages, now and forevermore! Amen" (Jude 24-25). God is ABLE to keep you from stumbling! And one day, He'll present you before His presence without fault—not because you were perfect, but because Jesus made you perfect—and with great joy!

## What We Learn from These Letters

1 John - God is love. You can't separate loving God from loving others! Real love acts. And you can KNOW you're saved! 2 John - Walk in both truth and love. Don't sacrifice one for the other! 3 John - Support faithful workers. Don't follow selfish leaders. Jude - Contend for the faith! But also build yourself up, pray, and stay close to God. God is able to keep you from stumbling!

Activity Time: Make a "Love in Action" challenge card. Draw a heart and divide it into 7 sections (one for each day). Each day this week, do one loving action (help someone, encourage a friend, serve your family). Write what you did in each section. At the end of the week, thank God for His love that empowers yours! For Parents: Read 1 John 4:7-10 about God's love. Discuss: "How did God show us what real love is?" (He sent Jesus to die for us when we didn't deserve it). Ask: "How can we show that kind of sacrificial love in our family?" Brainstorm practical ways to love others even when it costs us something.

# Chapter 20: The Grand Finale: Revelation and Your Ongoing Journey

You did it! You've journeyed through all 66 books of the Bible, from Genesis to Jude. Think about everything you've learned! You've read about creation and the fall, the flood and the exodus. You've met Abraham, Moses, David, and Daniel. You've heard the prophets promise a coming Messiah. And then you met Him—Jesus! You've learned about His miraculous birth, powerful teachings, amazing miracles, sacrificial death, and glorious resurrection. You've explored the early church and read Paul's letters about faith and grace. You've absorbed the wisdom of James, the hope of Peter, and the love of John. Now you're about to discover how the story ends. And spoiler alert: it's the best ending ever! The book of Revelation is the Bible's grand finale. It's filled with visions, symbols, angels, and epic battles between good and evil. Some parts might seem confusing, but the main message is crystal clear: Jesus wins! Evil is defeated, and God creates a new heaven and a new earth where His people will live with Him forever.

## What Is Revelation?

Revelation was written by John—the same John who walked with Jesus, who wrote the Gospel and three letters. But now John is an old man, probably in his early to mid-nineties, and he's been arrested and exiled by the Roman emperor Domitian during a brutal wave of Christian persecution. They've banished him to Patmos, a small, desolate, rocky island in the Aegean Sea used as a Roman penal colony for criminals and political prisoners. Imagine being that old, separated from all the churches you've poured your life into, isolated on a barren island with no way to teach or encourage believers. John must have felt lonely, wondering if this was how his life would end—alone on a rock in the middle of the sea. But that's exactly where Jesus met him in the most spectacular way! One Sunday morning—the Lord's Day—while John is worshiping, he suddenly hears behind him a loud voice like a trumpet blast commanding, "Write on a scroll what you see!" John turns around, and what he sees takes his breath away: seven golden lampstands, and among them is "someone like a son of man" clothed in a long robe with a golden sash. This is Jesus—but not the humble carpenter John once knew! Jesus' head and hair are white like wool, pure white as snow. His eyes blaze like flames of fire. His feet glow like bronze refined in a furnace. His voice sounds like a mighty waterfall or crashing ocean waves. In His right hand He holds seven stars, and a sharp double-edged sword comes from His mouth. And His face—His face shines like the sun at full strength! John, the disciple who once leaned against Jesus' chest at dinner, is so overwhelmed that he falls at Jesus' feet as though dead! But Jesus gently places His right hand on John and says with reassuring authority, "Do not be afraid. I am the First and the Last. I am the Living One; I was dead, and now look, I am alive for ever and ever! And I hold the keys of death and Hades" (Revelation 1:17-18). This is the risen, glorified, conquering Christ! Jesus told John to write down what he saw and send it to seven churches in Asia (modern-day Turkey). What follows is a breathtaking vision of the end times. Fun Fact: Revelation is the only Bible book that promises a special blessing to those who read it aloud and hear it! (Revelation 1:3)

## Letters to the Seven Churches

Revelation starts with messages to seven specific churches. These were real churches facing real challenges. Jesus knows exactly what's happening in each one. Some churches are praised for their hard work and faithfulness despite persecution. Others are rebuked for serious problems. The church in Ephesus has lost its first love—they're doing all the right things but their hearts have grown cold toward Jesus. The church in Laodicea is lukewarm, and Jesus says He's about to spit them out! Jesus calls each church to repent where needed and remain faithful. He promises amazing rewards to those who overcome: they'll eat from the tree of life, receive the crown of life, and sit with Jesus on His throne! These messages aren't just for those ancient churches—they're for us too! Which church sounds most like you? Are you passionate for Jesus or have you grown lukewarm? Think About It: - Jesus told the Ephesian church they'd lost their "first love." When did you love Jesus most? How can you get that passion back?

## The Throne Room of Heaven

In chapter 4, John sees God's throne room. It's breathtaking! God is seated on the throne, surrounded by brilliant light. Twenty-four elders and four living creatures worship Him, singing, "Holy, holy, holy is the Lord God Almighty!" Then John sees a scroll sealed with seven seals. No one is worthy to open it—except one: "the Lion of the tribe of Judah." But when John looks, he sees not a lion, but a Lamb who looks as if it had been slain. This is Jesus! He's both the conquering Lion and the sacrificial Lamb. All of heaven erupts in worship: "Worthy is the Lamb, who was slain, to receive power and wealth and wisdom and strength and honor and glory and praise!" (Revelation 5:12). Fun Fact: Revelation mentions worship and singing more than 20 times—heaven is filled with praise!

## The Seals, Trumpets, and Bowls

As Jesus opens the seals, judgments are poured out on the earth. Wars, famines, earthquakes, and cosmic disturbances. Then seven angels blow seven trumpets, bringing more judgments. Finally, seven bowls of God's wrath are poured out. These judgments are intense. They show that God takes sin seriously. But they also serve as warnings, giving people opportunities to repent. Throughout these visions, we also see God protecting His people. Revelation describes a dragon (Satan), two beasts (representing evil empires), and a city called Babylon (symbolizing the world system opposed to God). But their victory is short-lived. God judges Babylon. The beasts are thrown into the lake of fire. Satan is bound and eventually thrown into the lake of fire. Evil is completely defeated!

## The Return of Jesus

One of the most exciting parts is the description of Jesus' return. Revelation 19 describes Jesus riding a white horse, leading the armies of heaven. His name is "King of Kings and Lord of Lords." He comes to judge the earth and establish His kingdom. When Jesus returns, everything changes. The old order passes away, and a new order begins!

## A New Heaven and a New Earth

After the judgment, God creates something brand new. Not a renovated old earth—a completely new heaven and a new earth! The old creation, tainted by sin, passes away. God makes ALL things new! John sees the New Jerusalem, a beautiful city, coming down out of heaven. This is where God's people will live forever! The city is radiant with the glory of God, shining like a precious jewel. The walls are made of jasper. The city is pure gold. The foundations are decorated with precious stones. Each gate is a single pearl! And the main street is pure gold! But the most amazing thing about this city is that God dwells there with His people. Revelation 21:3-4 says, "Look! God's dwelling place is now among the people, and he will dwell with them. They will be his people, and God himself will be with them and be their God. 'He will wipe every tear from their eyes. There will be no more death' or mourning or crying or pain, for the old order of things has passed away." No more death! No more mourning! No more crying! No more pain! God will personally wipe away every tear! Can you imagine a world like that? There's no need for a temple, because God and the Lamb are the temple. There's no need for the sun or moon, because God's glory lights the city. The gates are never shut because there's no danger. The river of the water of life flows down the street, clear as crystal. On each side stands the tree of life—remember that from Genesis 3? It was in Eden, but after sin, humans were cut off from it. Now it's back! And the curse that began in Genesis 3 is finally, completely removed! Think About It: - In the New Jerusalem, God will wipe away every tear. What's something that makes you sad now? How does it feel to know that sadness won't last forever?

## Come, Lord Jesus!

Revelation ends with an invitation and a promise. Jesus says, "Look, I am coming soon!" (Revelation 22:7). The Spirit and the bride (the church) say, "Come!" Jesus is inviting people to come to Him and receive the water of life freely. And John responds with a prayer: "Come, Lord Jesus!" (Revelation 22:20). That's been the hope of Christians for 2,000 years. The Bible ends with a blessing: "The grace of the Lord Jesus be with God's people. Amen." Fun Fact: The Bible begins in a garden (Eden) and ends in a garden city (New Jerusalem)—God's plan comes full circle!

## Your Adventure Continues!

Congratulations! You've completed your journey through all 66 books of the Bible! This is a huge accomplishment! You've traveled from creation in Genesis to the new creation in Revelation. You've discovered how everything in the Bible points to Jesus! But here's the exciting part: this isn't the end—it's just the beginning! Think of this guide as a map for a great adventure. You've studied the map and discovered where the treasure is (Jesus!). Now it's time to actually go on the adventure! Here's how: Read your Bible regularly. Now that you know the big story, go back and read the actual books. Set a time each day—maybe 5-10 minutes—and make Bible reading a habit. Pray. Talk to God every day like you'd talk to a friend. Thank Him, ask for help, confess your sins, tell Him your dreams and fears. And be quiet and listen! Find a church. If you don't already have one, find a good church where the Bible is taught and Jesus is worshiped. You need Christian community! Share what you've learned. Tell your friends and family about Jesus. You're never too young to share your faith! Keep asking questions. If something confuses you, ask! Talk to a parent, pastor, or trusted Christian adult. Keep learning and growing! Live out your faith. This is the most important part! Don't just know about Jesus—follow Him! Let everything you learned change how you live. Love others the way Jesus loved. Serve those in need. Stand up for what's right. Be honest and kind. Let your life show that you belong to Jesus! Think About It: - You've learned so much about the Bible. What's one thing you want to remember most? How will it change how you live?

## The Story You're Part Of

Remember, you're not just reading someone else's story—you're part of it! God created a perfect world. Humans rebelled. But God had a plan from the beginning to rescue and restore humanity. He called Abraham, gave the Law, sent prophets, and then—at just the right time—He sent Jesus! Jesus lived the perfect life we couldn't live. He died the death we deserved. He rose from the dead, defeating sin and death forever. And now He's building His church. You're part of that family! You're part of God's kingdom! One day—maybe soon—Jesus will return. Evil will be judged. Death will be destroyed. And God will create a new heaven and a new earth where we'll live with Him forever. No more pain, no more tears, no more sin! Just perfect joy in God's presence for eternity! That's your future if you trust in Jesus! So keep following Jesus. Keep trusting Him even when life is hard. Keep running the race with perseverance. Keep your eyes fixed on the prize! You're not alone in this adventure. God is with you. The Holy Spirit lives inside you. You have the Bible to guide your steps. And you're surrounded by millions of believers running the same race! The adventure continues—and it's going to be amazing! God has great plans for you. So go live it! Be bold. Be faithful. Be courageous. Love people the way Jesus loves. Stand up for truth. Serve with joy. And keep following Jesus every single day! God bless you, friend. May you grow in the grace and knowledge of Jesus. May you experience His love more deeply. May you know His presence more fully. And may your life be a beautiful story of God's faithfulness and grace! The best is yet to come. Keep going! Jesus is worth it! Amen!

Activity Time: Create a "My Bible Journey" scrapbook page. Draw or write about your favorite Bible story, your favorite verse, one thing you learned, and one way you'll live differently. Add drawings or stickers. Keep it as a reminder of this amazing journey through God's Word! For Parents: Celebrate completing the Bible together! Have a special family dinner or dessert. Go around the table and share: (1) your favorite Bible story, (2) one thing you learned, and (3) one way you want to grow spiritually. Pray together, thanking God for His Word and asking Him to help your family live it out faithfully.

Printed in Dunstable, United Kingdom

78065694R00070